HOW TO INVEST IN REAL ESTATE

DISCOVER HOW TO CREATE WEALTH AND PASSIVE INCOME THROUGH REAL ESTATE INVESTING

Table of Contents

Introduction xi

Chapter 1: Overview of Real Estate Investment 1

Why You Should Invest in Real Estate 2
    It Is Safer, Easier, and Steady 2
    You Make Money Through Property Appreciation .. 2
    You Can Bargain on Pricing 3
    You Get Total Freedom 3
    You Can Invest in Different Ways 4
    There Is a Higher Demand for Houses
    Than the Supply 4
    It Is Easy to Get Financing 4

Can You Invest in Real Estate Without Any Money? 5

Can You Invest in Real Estate if You Have a
Full-Time Job? 6
    Income from Your Job Increases Growth in
    Your Investing Business 7
    A Job Will Get You Qualified for Bank Financing 8
    Ways to Invest Part-Time 8
    What It Takes to Invest in Real Estate When You
    Have a Full-Time Job 9
        Commitment 9
        Perseverance 10

Organization *11*
Hiring Out *12*
Can You Get Rich Quickly with Real Estate Investing? 13
Should You Pay a Real Estate Guru? 15

Chapter 2: The Cycle of Wealth **17**
Building Your Business Channel 17
Property Types and Investment Approaches 18
Multiple Income Streams 19
Portfolio Income 20
   Types of Portfolio Streams of Income
   in Real Estate 21
Distressed Properties vs. Motivated Sellers 22
Purchasing as Wholesale 25
   Analyzing Prospects 25
   Computing the Market Value 26
   Estimating Repairs 26
   Submitting Offers and Counter-Offers 26
   Getting Buyers 26
   How to Close Effectively 27
      Lease Options *27*
      Foreclosures *28*

**Chapter 3: Mastering Market Analysis
               and Evaluation** **29**
A Brief Recap of Past History — A Future Predictor 29
Real Estate Step-by-Step Market Analysis 30
   Why Is It Important to Perform Real
   Estate Market Analysis? 31
   How to Conduct Real Estate Market Analysis 32
      Check Location *32*

*Assess the Main Features of the
Investment Properties* 33
Compare the Data.. 34
The Bottom Line.. 34

Chapter 4: Understanding Your Market 35

Choose the Area You Want to Focus On........................... 37

Define Property Values Using Comps 38

What "Comparables" Mean... 39
Drive Near the Houses That Have Sold 42
Begin with the Roof.. 42
Check the Exterior of the House 42
Examine the Yard 43

Mastering Your Housing Market... 43

Be Active in the Community 43
Walk Around Your Communities 44
Create Local Content for Your Real Estate Blog...... 44

Fundamentals of Real Estate Market 45

Both Supply and Demand Establish Buyer's
and Seller's Markets....................................... 46
New Construction Expands the Supply..................... 47
Low Mortgage Rates Trigger Demand....................... 48
A Strong Economy Results in More Buyers.............. 48
The Average Price of Homes Reveals the
Housing Market's Direction 49

Chapter 5: Real Estate Niches and Strategies............ 51

Narrow Your Audience 51

Get Deeper 52

Be Authentic... 53

Become Hyperlocal 53

Create Your Own 53
Best Niches for Real Estate Investing and How to Select Yours 54
    Niches vs. Strategies 54
    Real Estate Investing Strategy 54
    Business Strategies 55
        Fix-and-flop 55
        Wholesaling 56
        Starter strategies 56
        Live-in-then-rent 56
        Live-in-flip 56
    Wealth-Building Strategies 57
        Short-term buy-and-hold 57
        Long-term buy and hold rentals 57
        Rental debt snowball plan 57
        All-cash rental plan 58
    Debt Strategies 58
        Hard money lending 58
        Discounted note investing 58
    Passive Income Strategies 59
        Syndications and crowdfunding 59
        Real estate investment trusts 59
    Property Niches 60
        Single-family houses 60
        Small apartment buildings 60
        Large apartment buildings 61
        Townhomes and condos 61
        Mobile homes on land 61
        Mobile home parks 62
        Land 62
        Private partnership 62
    Seller Niches 63

Property Seller Niches 63
End-User Niches 67
Location 70
City or town 70
Amenities, schools district, and neighborhoods 70

Chapter 6: Finding a Motivated Seller 71

Who Is a Motivated Seller? 72

How Do We Look for Them? 73
Teaming Up with Real Estate Experts 73
How to Work with More Than One Agent 74
Using Keywords 76
Expired Listings 76
Designing a Flyer to Attract Aggressive Agents 76
For Sale by Owner Signs 76
Looking for Vacant or Boarded Houses 77
Getting Owners of Vacant Houses 78
Auctions 79
Absolute auctions 79
Foreclosure auctions 80
FDIC, VA, IRS, and Many More 80
Garage Sales 80
Courthouse Records 81
Private Noteholders 81
Divorce Cases 82
Houses with Tax Liens 82
Out-of-State Owners 82
Bird Dogs 82
Signs 83
Bulletin Boards 83
Flyers 84
Handouts 84
Driving for Dollars 84

Cooperative Advertising..85
Direct Mail 85
Restrooms...85

Chapter 7: Real Estate Business Plan 86

Goals 87

Investment Strategy..87
    Type of Investment Property 88
    Real Estate Market..88

Financial Plan 88

Marketing Plan 89

Timeframe...89

Flexibility..90

Exit and Backup Plans 90

The Bottom Line 90

Chapter 8: Winning Financing 92

Become Creative...93

Working with Mortgage Brokers.....................................94

Contacting Mortgage Brokers...96
    Questions to Ask Mortgage Brokers 97

Seller Financing 100
    The Pros and Cons of Seller Financing....................102
        Drawbacks of Seller Financing from
        the Buyer's Perspective *103*
        Pros of Seller Financing from the
        Seller's Perspective *103*
        Drawbacks of Seller Financing from the
        Seller's Perspective *104*
    Tips for Seller Financing 105

Type of Owners Who Will Finance
Their Properties 106
The Bottom Line with Seller Financing 106

Due on Sale Clause and Land Trusts 107

Wraparound Mortgages 108

A Land Contract and Agreement for Deed 108

Other No- or Low-Money Techniques 109
Ignore the First Mortgage and Let the
Seller Carry a Second 109
The Owner Takes Back a Note 109
Split Funding 110
Balloon the Down Payment 110
Pay the Down Payment in Small Amounts 111
Subordination 111
Substitution of Collateral 112
Joint Venture with the Seller 112
Joint Venture with an Investor 112
Partners 113
Note *113*

Chapter 9: The Art of Negotiation 114

The Psychology of Negotiating 114

Detailed Knowledge of the Market 115

The Level of the Seller's Motivation 116

Backdoor Exits 119

Concessions 119

The Red Herring Approach 120

The Money-Talks Approach 120

How to Master Real Estate Negotiations 121
Negotiation Is Really an Art in Real Estate 121

Structure Your Offer for Acceptance........................122
　　The Home Inspection Is a Common
　　Negotiation Tool 123
　　Be Proactive and Not Reactive...................................123
　　Questions Results in Positive Answers
　　and Results 124
　　Real Estate Negotiation Techniques.........................124

Chapter 10: Secrets to Optimize Your Potential **127**

Post Entry Planning 127

DIY vs. Hiring It Out 128

Increasing the Marketability of Your Property...............129

Preplanning..129

Increasing Visibility Through the MLS 130

Selling a Marketable Product...................................131

Competitive Pricing...132

Offering Incentives..132

Building Your Winning Team of Experts.........................134
　　Scouts/Dealers 134
　　Office Manager..135
　　Property Rehab Manager..136
　　Mortgage Broker..137
　　Real Estate Attorney...137
　　Title Company 138
　　Real Estate Agents 138

Conclusion **139**

Introduction

Real estate investing has helped many people increase their net worth and manage to get the things that they always wanted to have, fulfill their financial goals faster than they thought it would be possible, and retain their wealth for their retirement.

It is worthy to note that many people have achieved the same without a lot of money. The fact is that real estate investing is a great tool for establishing and amassing wealth, regardless of where you live. Unlike other investment opportunities, real estate has a "staying power."

This book will take you through a step-by-step process to understand how to invest in real estate. Without further ado, let's dive in!

CHAPTER 1:

Overview of Real Estate Investment

Not everyone is going to get rich from their daily jobs. Some have a limited time for actively working. In order to reach financial independence, you have to look for more sources of passive income. Smart real estate investing can generate huge returns and increase your net worth.

Similar to stock investing, real estate investing can appear intimidating. However, that is not true. There are just some important things that you need to be aware of before you get started.

Regardless of how you take it, real property is here to stay, which is the reason why many decide to put their money into it. Investing in real estate has crossed in our minds at one point or another.

However, if this is an investment choice that you are considering, you might have no clue where to begin.

In order to succeed in property investment in the real estate market, you must first do your homework to make sure that you understand the small details of your local market, as well as the factors that define the profitability of what you are investing in.

Why You Should Invest in Real Estate

It Is Safer, Easier, and Steady

When you compare to other methods of earning income, real estate is the best because the industry is far less risky and volatile. It is a stable sector, especially for those investing in rental properties. As a real estate investor, you will continue to earn a stable stream of income through rental properties, even in a slow economy. People can switch to more affordable housing—but you will not sell fast, like in shares when things go wrong. Also, it's easy to invest in real estate compared to shares, start-up companies, or beginning your own business.

You Make Money Through Property Appreciation

Continuous income from tax-breaks and rent is good, but these are secondary reasons to invest in real estate. The value of your asset will increase over time. If you purchase your rental property using a mortgage, then it's probably your tenant who is going to pay back your loan plus interest to the bank. Over time, you will have a valuable asset to your name without $0 investment. Then, you can maintain the asset for the continuous stream of income that it generates or sell it for a higher price than what you purchased it for.

You Can Bargain on Pricing

When you invest in market shares, you will be purchasing or buying them based on the market price. You cannot bargain at its expense. Investing in real estate is different from this scenario. You can and should bargain for everything, which means better investment opportunities for you. As a savvy buyer, you can buy properties well below market price if you make use of your negotiation skills, market knowledge, and professional network. If you are going to flip houses for a living, then you can sell that house for a higher price than market value if you play your game right.

You Get Total Freedom

One of the reasons why people decide to invest in real estate is because of the freedom that one gets from it. You have the chance to manage the properties yourself or hire a property manager to handle everything for you.

As an investor, you will have sufficient freedom to do things that will increase your cash flow.

In real estate, the success of your property is mostly determined by yourself. If you want more money, then you need to hustle hard.

You Can Invest in Different Ways

Real estate is a flexible industry based on investment options. It provides something to everyone.

Whether you want to invest for short-term gain or you are in this for a long-haul, you will get an investment strategy right for your financial goals.

There Is a Higher Demand for Houses Than the Supply

Apartments are always in demand, especially when the world's population continues to increase. A gap exists between the supply and demand for real estate. As such, if you invest in the correct property based on the demands of people, you can make a good profit even when the real estate market seems down.

It Is Easy to Get Financing

Banks like real estate. That is the main reason why home loans are a major part of their business model. As an investor, it is going to be a lot easier to get financing for residential properties than any other asset class.

Since real estate has a special place in the heart of lenders and banks, you can borrow more money from them using your house as leverage. Typically, you can attain 80 to 90% of home equity as a loan, but the credit score plays a significant role in defining how much you will earn.

But still, this is far more than what lenders may provide you against, say, for instance, a share portfolio.

Can You Invest in Real Estate Without Any Money?

The simple answer is yes. The ability to recognize and take advantage of other people's money is the trait of successful real estate investors. Why? They have learned the art of investing in real estate with no cash of their own. For newer and financially strapped investors, this is the best way to get a foot in the real estate door without the financial resources and credit to do so. Skilled and experienced investors in this field have discovered that relying on other people's cash liquidates their available cash and allows them to invest more, and make more.

Investing in real estate without using any of your money is the most complex but vital tools you can build in your real estate career.

The secret to investing in real estate without any money of your own is to bring something to the table. If you don't have cash, there are many other things that you can contribute to the deal. Many investors use little of their money while investing in real estate by relying on methods such as:

- Partners
- Lease option strategies
- Wholesaling
- Home equity loans
- Private or hard money
- *And many more!*

We will look at each of these methods in detail later in this book, but we want you to know that investing in real estate without income is possible, but it might not be as easy as many online gurus put it.

There is no doubt about it: investing with no or little money is possible. You don't need big cash reserves of your own to get a deal. You only need to know how to invest in properties with the right people at your side.

Can You Invest in Real Estate if You Have a Full-Time Job?

Many people think that to be successful, and they need to quit their main jobs and focus on real estate investing permanently. It is a complex decision to make because there are many benefits to maintaining your job as well as drawbacks to consider.

Yes. It is possible to invest in real estate if you have a full-time job. Remember, there are different ways to make money in real estate, and every strategy and approach requires a different amount of time.

Some methods may involve you being active in your business and demand 40-hour workweeks. Other methods can be more passive and demand 40 hours all year.

The good thing about real estate is that there are different ways at hand that you can go for.

Income from Your Job Increases Growth in Your Investing Business

One of the greatest reasons to invest in real estate while going about with your main job is that your job can generate the income required to fund your investment business.

Depending on the amount of money you save, you will have money every year to grow your real estate investments.

You will also manage to reinvest the money from your investments because you will have your job income to boost your cost of living.

A person who invests full time and has no other job may experience slower growth because they have to use the income from their investments to fund living expenses.

A Job Will Get You Qualified for Bank Financing

Another great reason to maintain your job when you are first starting in real estate investing is the availability of bank financing.

To acquire a loan from a bank, you need to show evidence of income and have a better credit score.

Your job will be proof of income that gets you approved for bank financing.

On many occasions, investors and entrepreneurs who don't have a job and are full-time real estate, find it difficult to get loans from banks because their business does not generate sufficient income or they lack 2-3 years of proof of continuous income.

Your job will be a powerful tool in the early stages of your investing business until the ball gets rolling and your business runs well to allow you to quit.

Ways to Invest Part-Time

- Purchase rental property and employ a property manager.

- Link up with larger investment deals as a limited partner.
- Invest in notes.
- Act as a hard or private money lender to other real estate investors.

Real estate can be highly profitable regardless of which way you to take it. However, that doesn't mean that you quit your main job and become a full-time investor because you have read about other investors who did that way. Having a detailed plan for how you want to move forward in real estate is important. In general, if you hate your job, then make decisions on how well off your current financial situation is in helping you to become a full-time real estate investor.

What It Takes to Invest in Real Estate When You Have a Full-Time Job

If you are planning to invest in real estate while maintaining a permanent job, don't worry—*you are not alone*. Many top investors started precisely the same way. If you are worried about how you are going to manage a real estate when you already have a 9-5 job, here are tips to help you learn how to get it all done:

Commitment

Like any other goal, if you are not 100 percent committed, you are never going to succeed.

When it comes to real estate investing, the same applies. Commitment is one of the most critical factors. Getting started in real estate investing is like starting a business from square zero. You will need to research, create a business plan, visit properties, call house owners, and follow leads.

How you dedicate your time to all this is up to you and significant to your situation.

Do you use your short breaks to complete these tasks? Do you wake up early or stay up late? Do you take vacation time? Everyone has a unique situation, and only you can make these decisions.

Either way, you can make use of your time to get started in real estate investment. While this might look like a huge sacrifice, consider the benefit you will get from getting started right away.

Perseverance

Things will not always go your way: you may fail to get bids on time, schedules may not line up, and you may fail to visit properties right way.

In the real estate market, things happen quickly, and those with a full-time job as well as pre-planned schedules to work around may lack the upper hand in these situations.

Sometimes, you may get time to visit a location, but the property does not fit your standards, or you might find a property that does not fulfill your return on investment (ROI) goals once you finish your research.

Be ready to spend time tracking leads that may not work out, and be ready to come across locations that may already have offered before you can get to them.

That is the nature of the market. However, with perseverance, you can finally get gold.

<u>Organization</u>

When you have a full-time job, you are already busy. So when you include real estate investing to the mix, things get a bit hectic.

The right way to deal with the situation is to stay on top of things and remain organized by putting systems and schedules into place.

You have a limited time, so arranging it is important for getting the most out of your new venture. You don't want to waste time looking for names, phone numbers, or papers. Set notification on your phone, leave notes in places that you know you will find them, and maintain an organized plan and do whatever else allows you to keep things together and easy to sort through.

This process of scheduling balances your time. Since you will be committing most of your personal time to your new project, it is easy to be swept away and be over-involved.

Losing family time or time for your hobbies can make you get burned out fast and possibly leave the project before you even invest fully.

Set a schedule for yourself to avoid this.

Creating a balance will allow you to avoid being overwhelmed or stressed, and it will prevent any mistakes or quick decisions that might potentially cost you money in the long-term.

<u>Hiring Out</u>

Recruiting can be a big lifesaver when you have a 9-5 job and invest in real estate.

There are many dimensions of the real estate investment process that can be used as a third party, letting you remain committed to your full-time job or uphold obligations to your family.

Get a virtual assistant to discuss the purchase price, or spend money on an excellent investment agent that can identify valuable properties. In some instances, these investment agents can deal with all aspects of the process for you. They can search, schedule showings and closes, and file all legal paperwork for you.

Certain agencies deliver property management services, making you remain hands-off even after closing your deal. They can facilitate tenant selection and retention, 24-hour maintenance, and all legal issues that might arise during ownership.

During the closing process, employing inspectors and assessors will protect you from investing in a possible money pit, because they can identify costly repairs early.

Renovations and repairs can all be delegated to contractors. You also have the option to seek a property management company that can handle these services for you.

Although it might cost you money upfront, hiring personnel helps you to balance your part-time investing, family life, and full-time work. This is the most important element to get started in real estate investing while maintaining a full-time job.

Can You Get Rich Quickly with Real Estate Investing?

There is no question, one of the major draws to real estate investing is the notion that investors drive big cars, live in large homes, and they are very wealthy. Although a lot of real estate investors amass a lot of wealth in their careers, real estate investment is not a "get rich quick" scheme.

Yes, few make a lot of money in a short period; but these instances are rare to find.

Sorry if you thought real estate could make you productive overnight.

Well, investing in real estate requires patience, proper planning, and persistence. Don't expect to reap millions of dollars in your first year; you will be left disappointed.

Instead, make plans on building a real estate that will slowly grow every year to allow you to fulfill your financial goals-and hopefully make your dreams a reality.

Regardless of what you may hear, being successful in real estate demands hard work. It is also important to keep in mind that there are no products, shortcuts, or tools that will complete the work for you. You must be ready to learn the rubrics and then apply them.

Real estate is the fastest method to generate wealth in the modern world. If done right, real estate can supercharge your growth because of the great power of leverage and the ability to hustle.

Should You Pay a Real Estate Guru?

Many newbies in real estate investing are convinced into getting a real estate guru who promises to teach them how to become successful-for a certain fee.

In most cases, these real estate gurus offer lower-cost first workshops about flipping houses. Well, are they worth it?

Overall, those new to the industry of real estate should be cautious when paying thousands of dollars for any guru program.

The bottom line on these programs is that a lot is required to being a successful real estate investor than mastering a slick system from a coach.

Here are the five major realities of real estate investing success:

- It takes a lot of work to become successful in this niche.

- Most aspiring real estate investors don't even do a deal, let alone make any money at it.

- The biggest part of being a successful long-term investor arises from establishing a stellar reputation in your market.

- Success in investing does arise from creating a proven team of real estate professionals at good prices, including agents, rehabbers, title companies, and many more.

- Most successful investors are professionals in their local area, and that requires years of work.

As you can see, none of these can be taught by a real estate investing coach in five or 10 days.

Keep in mind that real estate gurus are in the business of marketing and selling you on the dream. This book plus thousands of articles, and hundreds of discussions available online will help you learn everything that you don't need to pay thousands of dollars to a guru for.

CHAPTER 2:

The Cycle of Wealth

Building Your Business Channel

If you plan to travel from New York City to San Francisco, you will see good road signs that will guide you to find your way without using a comprehensive road map that describes your journey.

The same applies when you decide to invest in the business. If you have a clear picture of the benefits and advantages of different kinds of real estate deals, assessing your current position in terms of resources, as well as moving in the right direction with the least amount of wasted time, it will be a major asset to you. This is the focus of this chapter—to help you start to see where you are, where you want to go, and the right way to get there.

The first thing you need to do is to review your financial evaluation at this moment in time. Is your credit strong or weak?

Do you have access to money lending avenues? Are private and public lenders ready to help you get started? Once you have clearly examined your current status, you are okay to start selecting the right kind of deals to push you towards financial freedom. For instance, if you have smaller credit resources, you will want to select real estate deals that do not depend on either credit or funding.

One of these deals is "wholesaling."

Hence, let's start this chapter by exploring the different methods to make money, as well as the type of money needed to accomplish that kind of deal.

Property Types and Investment Approaches

Real estate investing is a great investment because of the many property types that one can invest in, plus techniques for what to do with those properties. And each has its own rewards.

Investors factor different options depending on the result they want to accomplish, the amount of money they want to invest in the project, and their level of experience with various strategies.

For instance, an investor might want to go for quick cash investment methods for different reasons, among them lack of enough capital to work with, or high consumer debt.

Multiple income channels and opportunities demand the right knowledge to specialize in different parts.

Multiple Income Streams

You could be wondering how to select your streams of income and what factors should dictate your decision. Here's a list of the different types of income:

- Wholesaling
- Probate
- Remodeling
- Rehabbing
- Land development
- Discount note selling
- Foreclosures

Meanwhile, here are some passive streams of income in real estate:

- Leases
- Property management
- Recreational parks

- Rentals
- Apartment houses
- Mobile home parks

In general, anything that you will contract and sell quickly falls into earned income.

Passive income refers to money that you get week after week, or monthly without you going out and doing another deal. As a result, passive income is sometimes called a recurring income.

When it comes to real estate, properties that fall under passive streams of income are your buy and hold rentals. Once you close on these deals, you collect rent every single month. Another real estate field that can be considered passive is when you become a property manager, or you own a property management company, and investors use you to collect the rents for them and pay you some fee for doing it.

Portfolio Income

Here is when your money starts to generate money for you, especially through interest.

There are different ways to generate portfolio income that is real estate related. Most of these methods of income relate to the investor earning interest on his or her money. While this chapter will not dig much into these methods, it is critical for you to understand the definition of these income streams.

Types of Portfolio Streams of Income in Real Estate

Real estate can help investors build wealth through a systematic channel that builds upon itself.

While everyone is different with different demands and goals on their time, professional real estate investors will always want to between 3-5 streams of earned income, and 2-3 streams of portfolio income.

New investors that have a limited amount of money start by being knowledgeable in various earned income streams like foreclosure, wholesale, and rehabbing. Now, they have a lot of freedom over their potential to generate huge amounts of cash in a short period of time. Next, they take that money and begin to invest in buy and hold properties.

As the passive income increases or the lease option properties grows, the investor has two choices to make: either purchase another buy and hold property or invest in a portfolio stream.

Distressed Properties vs. Motivated Sellers

There is an old saying about real estate investing that goes, "There are only two types of deals out there, distressed properties or distressed sellers."

No matter your investment strategy, you will realize that certain properties have a higher ideal investment opportunity than others.

Professional investors compare each deal against a set of merits and consider the benefits of that type of deal versus the opportunities present. They don't always fulfill each characteristic defined, but they assess and make informed decisions.

When evaluating a distressed property, look for the following advantages:

- There is minimal competition for them because the average individual wants properties in the best condition.

- You can always buy distressed properties under flexible, easy terms and for prices relatively below the market value.

- You have the freedom to heighten the value through smaller improvements and rehab work.

- A lot of market areas have many distressed properties to select from.

Some things to consider about distressed properties include:

- Many real estate markets have a certain number of investors searching for this type of properties, so your marketing efforts should be active, well-organized, and effective to discover better deals. It can be great to investigate different marketing strategies that have done well for other real estate investors.

- In order to avoid costly mistakes, you must know how to examine the property and its neighborhood accurately.

- Through inspections and repairs, estimates have to be done before the purchase.

- If the property is located in a lower-income neighborhood, the comparable sales in that particular place will surpass a specific amount of money, regardless of how change is done. Repairs are usually costly. In order to optimize profitability in the older, lower-income areas, it is safe to integrate a distressed property with a distressed seller and take advantage of the profit potential on every aspect.

Meanwhile, here are the pros of working with distressed sellers:

- There is seller distress in each price range.

- Sometimes, you can buy properties under flexible and easy terms. The seller requires help, and in most cases, just wants a way out, but does not know what to do. You can offer a solution.

- Seller distress often results from property distress, so the opportunities of being able to increase property value through cosmetic changes or rehabbing when you can connect a distressed seller with a distressed property are great.

- You must know what caused the seller to experience the situation they are in and find out the best way to help them get out of it. To understand their problem and find the best solution, you must develop good listening and negotiation skills.

- Certain distressed sellers give compelling reasons why they want to remain in their properties, and the tendency is to want to accommodate this. If their problem is for financial reasons, this can be risky. It is relevant to keep your emotions out of it.

Purchasing as Wholesale

Distressed properties are the best option for wholesaling candidates. And wholesaling is a great opportunity because it requires the least expertise and is the kind of deal new investors want.

Wholesale deals might be one of the first types of deals you will make in real estate investing because you stand a great chance to land distressed properties.

In order to succeed with wholesaling, some of the things that you need to know do include how to segment your market correctly, how to create a database of possible properties, and many more. Also, you need to understand a few basic elements of the wholesaling business, including:

Analyzing Prospects

Because distressed properties should be your main target, you must learn how to identify and review distressed homes. You also need to understand that a distressed property doesn't imply that a deal is good, but that it is a great start. So you need to memorize the techniques to help you know when a deal is too good to be true, when it is the right time to move forward, and when the deal needs to be left on the table.

Computing the Market Value

You must know the significance of calculating fair market value after repairs to succeed as a wholesaler. The real estate experts on your power team will be a valuable asset for finding this information. Also, by using comparable sales of properties in the same location will allow you to know the market value.

Estimating Repairs

This will not be a successful process if you fail to approximate repairs correctly. Learn how to check deals to make sure you present an offer that will lead to the highest profit. There are also techniques you can learn that will save you cash on rehab projects and optimize your profits.

Submitting Offers and Counter-Offers

You have to become familiar with good communication and negotiating skills, learn how to submit offers and counteroffers without destroying your goals, and learn how to manage contracts. Understanding how to properly review properties will be significant in determining what to offer and whether you need to make an offer.

Getting Buyers

Wholesaling is half-done when you can find deals and bargain, but there is no one to assign contracts to.

Creating a sizable investor database to tap no matter the kind of deal you are working on will assist you in moving things forward quickly and maintain your profit margins.

How to Close Effectively

It is important you learn the right ways to close without money.

Lease Options

The lease is one of the most interesting real estate investment opportunities for both new and experienced investors because they can produce multiple income streams within a single deal. Here are some general points you need to know about lease options in real estate: if you purchase a property using a lease option, you can:

- Interact with distressed sellers and not distressed properties. Circumstances of the seller create the deal. What you need to do is to identify the problem owners.

- Acquire freedom of a property without taking ownership. You are not mandated to buy, but you have attained the right to purchase.

- Manage nice homes in great places. In this case, the seller needs to get out, and the investor gets in. Better neighborhood increases demand.

- Help another person in different ways. The defining aspect of lease options is always debt relief. You are always working with people who might not want to sell their property, but who have to sell it because of financial issues. Thus, you can help someone find a solution quickly. Similarly, you can do it with or without any money.

Foreclosures

The foreclosure market can be a great channel for making a profit both for new and experienced investors. Foreclosure happens every day, and this can be your chance not to grab a wise investment, but also help someone in need.

Keep in mind that foreclosures can happen for various reasons, and this is a niche where you can achieve a win-win scenario and do something that assists both you and the individual in need. Investors must be able to negotiate well with both lenders and homeowners to boost profits on these deals.

With multiple strategies to use and ways to generate money in real estate, knowledge will be a vital factor for you to succeed.

By reviewing the available opportunities in real estate investing, you will have completed your first critical step towards achieving financial independence. Now, is the time to proceed to the next level.

CHAPTER 3:

Mastering Market Analysis and Evaluation

A Brief Recap of Past History — A Future Predictor

The challenge with this kind of reaction is the paper currency we use in the U.S. The way the economy grows is for the paper to keep circulating. Thus, when the flow of money stops, the economy begins to stall.

In order to motivate people to spend their money and keep the paper currency circulating, the Federal Reserve decreased the interest rates, which allowed people to purchase properties with far less interest expense than historic levels had required. Also, loan programs were released with lenient rules so that many people could qualify for loans.

Now, with the stock market in a stagnating condition, average home interest rates lower than they had been in the past thirty years, and lending rules more lenient than it had even been, people started to purchase homes and land.

Hence, real estate became the best investment choice for people who had never owned a home at all. Adding to that, investors who were afraid of the stock market performance started to pull available revenue from this kind of investing and direct it to real estate.

Besides the trigger of low-interest rates and relaxed lending qualifications, the first signs of baby-boomers were about to retire. As they saw the chance to invest, they started to visit retirement states and buy their homes earlier than they had arranged. This was a smart move on their part-but it triggered a rise in demand on real estate that was unexpected.

When opportunities to make money arise, builders will emerge to take advantage of the opportunity.

Because there were enough homes available to buy, plans for construction were the norm.

Real Estate Step-by-Step Market Analysis

Getting rich is normally the focus behind becoming a real estate investor. But the journey starts with learning about real estate topics like how to carry out real estate market analysis. Investment property analysis is one of the leading things that beginner real estate investors must learn. It is not that complicated, and with proper guidance, you will fully understand what it takes to conduct a real estate market analysis when buying or selling an investment property.

This section will expand more on real estate market analysis.

Why Is It Important to Perform Real Estate Market Analysis?

This is one of the most critical steps for a beginner to experienced investors. The reason, it allows them to understand the estimated value of the income property they want to purchase, sell, or rent out.

Analysis of investment property helps you know the current housing market condition and how much investment properties similar to yours are important. For that reason, if you want to rent out your property, market analysis helps you know in advance the amount to charge.

By creating a comparison of your investment property to other similar homes on the market, it is easy to set a price on your rental property.

But it is important to keep in mind that the current market listings aren't 100% correct, because they are subject to estimation. It is important to highlight that the seller's market focuses on the highest prices, while the buyer's market focuses on the least prices when it comes to investment property values.

How to Conduct Real Estate Market Analysis

Investing in real estate demands specific knowledge of the real estate investor's local housing market. As a seller, landlord, property buyer, concentrating on investment properties similar to your target property in the same location can be helpful and will provide realistic data on what you need to expect when you rent your property, presenting an offer on a property, or listing your house on the market.

Well, how do you conduct real estate market analysis?

Check Location

Location is one of the most important elements in the field of real estate investment. Every property's worth is defined by its location. In the case of investment property analysis, location is very critical because of the following reasons. First, conducting real estate market analysis requires that the subject property should be compared with other similar properties in the same area. Secondly, the property should be in an attractive area of great value. But this does not mean that location is the only thing that is important when investing in a property, but it is one of the most significant features.

A house near to public transport, main roads, business centers, and public amenities for sure is a very lucrative investment in your local housing market. To determine an estimated value of such a house, you will need to compare it with the prices of other investment properties around that area in the last 6 months.

As critical as it is the location of an investment property, it is not the only thing to consider when doing a real estate market analysis. So let us jump to the next feature in property investment analysis.

Assess the Main Features of the Investment Properties

Any buyer who wants to invest in a property has to consider the main characteristics that define whether the investment property is worth the money or not. The property seller also considers these features in his or her property to define its price.

These features comprise of house age, the number of floors, bathrooms, and bedrooms.

Performing a real estate market analysis involves reviewing amenities such as fireplaces, pools, major heating systems, and so forth. It is also important to mention all the recent improvements done to the house, as they play a key role in ensuring the house looks appealing to potential buyers. Once this is done, you search for houses with similar characteristics.

Once you compare your property to similar ones in the same area currently on the market or sold recently, you can look where your property fits within the range of prices.

Compare the Data

There are two major non-physical characteristics that are considered in real estate market analysis: price per square foot and vacancy rate.

The Bottom Line

Getting wealthy by investing in real estate isn't a pipe dream. In fact, it is likely to take place with the correct knowledge and management. Real estate market analysis is among the things that new real estate investors must enrich themselves to set their first steps in the niche of real estate investments.

CHAPTER 4:

Understanding Your Market

As learned in the previous chapter, real estate investors must understand how to analyze the entire market to understand what is happening within it at any given moment. Also, they must apply their knowledge to identify the highest profitable neighborhoods within that market for their different streams of income.

Now, with that particular knowledge, we can start to look at methods to make wise purchasing decisions in the correct places.

The most critical thing you will perform in real estate investing is to buy right and create the best deal possible when purchasing a property. This is where you will generate your cash in real estate. In fact, you may have heard people say it before: you make your money when you purchase; you only notice it when you sell your property and generate profit, or when you begin getting positive cash flow from an income-generating property.

And it's true. Thus, it is important you make the right purchase—this means you don't pay too much for a property.

In order to achieve this, you must know and understand the market you are buying in. After all, the only method you can compute the after-repair value of a property is by understanding the fair market value of properties in the area you select to focus. It is an important step in the evaluation process.

Some people believe that the correct market value is what they see advertised in the classified section of the newspaper, or in flyers they removed from the box on a real estate agent's sign. However, that is a "wish list"- what the seller expects to get. The correct market value is not what people ask for. It is what someone is ready to pay, and someone else is ready to accept. And more specifically, the sales prices of houses that have been sold within the last six months.

Regardless of the type of real estate investing you do, lease option, foreclosure, or income property, you will require to understand your market. Knowing your market will allow you to know what to quote as your offer, how to identify the best deal when you see one, and how to respond quickly. And as you increase your knowledge of the market, you will be spending less time searching for properties that are not the best investments.

Start by finding out in a low-to-moderate-income neighborhood, where you will see a huge inventory of properties. If you would like to purchase, fix, and sell, search for decent neighborhoods where it is obvious neighbors are concerned about their property and the community.

If you want to wholesale properties, you will be focusing a lot on distressed properties.

Of course, to define your target area in connection to your goals, you need to understand the location of these areas in your city. If you aren't sure where these areas are, you will have to segment your city with the assistance of your real estate agent. If you don't have a real estate professional, then you will need to get one.

As you continue to be familiar with real estate investing and the skills you need for the streams of income you concentrate, you will start to make great deals.

You will also know how to search for properties.

Choose the Area You Want to Focus On

Pick a place you want to concentrate on. Your target area depends on the type of investing you want to do.

For instance, if you want to purchase a house, fix it up, and resell it, you will be searching in the working to middle-income locations. If you want to carry out quick-turns without ever fixing the property, you will search in the places that are more distressed. Locations that rehabbers like to work in. If you are not sure which location to focus, then begin with the working to middle-income neighborhoods. You can always expand to other places.

Once you finish this assignment, you will manage to go to another region, anywhere in the country, and get to understand the market there quickly.

Define Property Values Using Comps

Once you choose your target location, you are ready to learn the market. You can ask a real estate agent to retrieve the comps around the neighborhood. You will need to have a list of properties that have been sold in the past six months in that neighborhood you want to invest. You need the agent to help you with this because comps create a chance for you to understand the market.

Some people assume that the exact market is what they advertised in newspapers. However, the correct market value is what a person wants to pay, and another person is ready to accept in an open market.

Real estate compares prices to identify properties that have been sold in square footage, number of bedrooms, number of amenities to the house they want to appraise, and many more.

Appraisers will always consider three houses and compute the value of the house they are appraising depending on the recent sales prices for those similar houses. Appraisers still consider other methods to compute the value of a property like a cost replacement method. With the above method, they compare this house to what it would cost per square foot to establish a new one. However, this method is not accurate because of supply and demand, plus the economics of a place define what people are ready to pay. You will discover the appraised value relies heavily on the comparables.

On the other hand, if the agent retrieves 40 houses, that's too many. Request your agent to compress the list down either by square footage, geography, and the number of bedrooms until you have 20 houses.

Remember that details about houses that have sold within the last three months are important than the comps that are six months old because the market can change very quickly.

What "Comparables" Mean

When you look at the list of properties that have been sold in the last six months, you will discover information about every house, such as:

- Listed price: This is the price the house was defined for.

- Sold Price: This is the price the house is sold for.

- Days on the market: This refers to the number of days listed to this, it shows how many days the home has been on the market before it was eventually sold. Sometimes, you will see a number representing the number of days it takes to sell the property. Other times, you might see both listed and sold date. Either way, this delivers valuable information because it allows you to understand the time it takes to sell a house in your area.

- Square footage: This describes the size of the house. It also helps define the cost per square foot that homes are selling for.

- How many bedrooms and baths

- Lot size: This may indicate the dimension of the lot or describe the percent of an acre the lot is.

- Year established or the age of house: This shows the year the house was built or how old the house is.

This is the least information you need to have on every comp. However, you will perhaps see more because you are going to request the agent to include remarks and a picture. Why the remarks are so crucial is you will be attempting to determine why these houses sold for the price they sold for. You will only drive by each of them, but since they have been sold, you will not be allowed to see inside. Since you cannot judge a house by its outside appearance, the remarks will show the condition of the house.

Some of the things that you might see on the remark section of the MLS include:

- Need TLC
- Great Fixer-Upper
- Sold As-Is
- Handyman special

When you read this, you will quickly tell that the house requires some work even if it looks beautiful outside.

Additional things that you might find in the remarks section include:

- Divorce
- Motivated seller
- Bank owned

- Must sell
- Illness-forced sales
- Transferred

When you come across these words, it could be a sign the seller is motivated.

Drive Near the Houses That Have Sold

Once you have your list of comparables, next is to drive by each of the houses on it. Stop the car and look through the window. Write down whatever you see. This is not a test to identify something wrong with the property. The house might look beautiful. You are only trying to find out why the house sold for that price.

Begin with the Roof

How does the roof appear? You don't need to be a roofing expert to know that it needs work if you notice some missing shingles.

Check the Exterior of the House

How does it look? Does it need some work? Again, this is not a test to determine something wrong with the house. You have the freedom to write down, "House looks great." But in case you find something is wrong, then write it down. Make sure you focus on the MLS pictures.

In case the pictures don't look great, then the individual that purchased the house perhaps fixed it up.

Examine the Yard

How does the yard look? Does it look like it is taken care of? Again, pay attention to the picture.

Mastering Your Housing Market

Purchasing a house is interesting (and sometimes, a bit complicated). If you are like many home shoppers, you can spend close to three months searching for your home.

You may find what looks like the perfect place, only to discover that it's beyond your target price.

Despite this, there are a few home hacks that can help you make a smart purchase. It all begins with researching your market.

Here are tips to help you understand the market well:

Be Active in the Community

You might be already active in your local community. If yes, ensure you share your interests and connections on your website. You don't know what may trigger a conversation or cause a potential buyer to pick up the phone and call you.

If you are not involved, then get active in the community. Participating in the community not only makes you popular, but it also allows you to understand what is taking place around town and helps you share those experiences, and that knowledge.

Walk Around Your Communities

The best way to learn about neighborhoods in your local real estate market is to get out and tour around the neighborhoods. Walk to the new development found on the outskirts of town and look around them. Understand the street names. Master the quickest routes from every neighborhood to the airport. Understand the differences among the local grocery stores, coffee shops, and bakeries.

Create Local Content for Your Real Estate Blog

Your website is a great place to begin establishing your credentials as a local real estate market expert. In case your website or blog features content that helps potential prospects discover more about your community, you will attract visitors to your site and establish yourself as a market leader.

Creating content doesn't have to take a lot of time. If you have recently attended a local event, you can update your website with pictures of the said event and some short descriptions about why events like these make your community a wonderful place to live.

Fundamentals of Real Estate Market

As said earlier, having enough knowledge of the real estate market makes you a powerful seller or buyer.

This section will focus on the five aspects that impact the market and how they affect your purchasing and selling power. They comprise:

- Median home prices
- Mortgage rates
- Economy
- New construction
- Supply and demand

For buyers, being aware of these factors can help you define your negotiating and purchasing ability.

For sellers, it can allow you to set the price of your home and predict the number of offers and selling timeline.

Both Supply and Demand Establish Buyer's and Seller's Markets

A neighborhood may have many properties, but only a small section is for sale at any given time. The supply of for-sale properties relative to the demand to purchase them determines whether the market supports buyers or sellers.

A buyer's market is one where there are many homes available for sale, but not many people want to purchase. On the other hand, a seller's market is one where many people want to buy homes, but the homes are scarce.

If you purchase in a buyer's market, it shows that you have a lot of power. You can be lucky to find a lower price and a nice closing date. The seller could pay some of your closing costs or wait to close until your current home.

It can be difficult to buy in a seller's market. The seller may get numerous offers. If a home is attractive, there will be a bidding competition to shoot the price up. You may be required to agree to whatever terms the seller is interested in, even if they are costly for you.

Managing to sell in a seller's market shows the amount of power you have, you could get different offers for more than your asking price. You will always manage to determine the terms you want. You may not need to fix up your property to sell it.

Keep in mind that it can be difficult to sell in a buyer's market. You may not find the price you want or the price you found some months ago for a property that is similar to yours. You may need to make a lot of repairs and improvements to your house before you get an interested buyer.

The National Association of Realtors(NAR) is a trade organization for realty brokers. This is an excellent place for housing market data. The association monitors the volume of closed and pending sales of available properties in a major metropolitan area. Data and analysis are released monthly, and the association economists apply important insights into current supply and demand needs in the nation's housing markets.

Most local realtor groups and multiple-listing services release local housing market data and analyses that can allow you to master the market dynamics.

New Construction Expands the Supply

Existing houses are not the only source of supply of homes for sale. Homes exist on the market when they are presented by new-home builders.

Newly built houses cost more than similar resale homes. That difference exists because of the following:

- Adhere to the current building codes for structural and safety soundness.

- Do demand less maintenance in the near term.

- They are normally energy –efficient than older homes.

Low Mortgage Rates Trigger Demand

Mortgage rates affect housing markets indirectly because the rates of interest are a main aspect of the demand to buy homes.

When rates increase, financing a home purchase becomes expensive, reducing the demand to purchase. The opposite effect happens when rates are decreasing. As financing becomes cheap, more people choose to purchase a home instead of rent.

Most people think that the Federal Reserve defines mortgage interest rates. But that isn't true.

The mortgage rates that homebuyers and homeowners do shell out are established by banks, mortgage companies, and credit unions.

A Strong Economy Results in More Buyers

Other economic factors such as job creation, wage growth, employment, and household formation also affect demand for houses.

The Average Price of Homes Reveals the Housing Market's Direction

The average price of homes is a great sign of the direction of real estate markets. However, this data has to be analyzed with caution.

While it is tempting to monitor monthly, or quarterly average price trends, the correct comparison is in the same time period last year. And that is because sales and prices are affected by seasonality.

Many housing markets are categorized by price bands. In certain markets, high-priced homes are divided into two markets: multimillion-dollar and million-dollar.

These market divisions are critical because middle prices can be skewed by changes in the mix of homes sold. In case that a large number of luxury homes are sold in a particular area during a given period, the middle price may rise in case the general prices were flat.

Median prices can reveal the direction of housing markets over time. This information can be very useful for sellers and buyers.

Buying when prices are going up can be frustrating. One problem that prices of recently sold comparable homes may not be a great reflector of current home values is because of the rapid speed of home price appreciation. In a lucrative market, buyers will face stiff competition and will require to submit a bid above the asking price.

Decreasing prices boost buyer purchasing ability. You can manage to purchase a larger or better home or one in a more desirable place for less than you would previously have paid.

Selling when prices are soaring high can be the best thing. You could be able to list for higher or earn higher offers than you expected.

Selling when prices reduce can be challenging. You may have to agree for a lower price and sell your home at a lower price than other comparable sales data.

Mastering these housing market fundamentals motivates both buyers and sellers to make smart decisions related to buying or selling a home.

CHAPTER 5:

Real Estate Niches and Strategies

Nowadays, it is not enough to market yourself as a "local real estate expert." Consumers have first-time access to experiences that suit their special needs and choices, and real estate is not different.

In this competitive world, successful agents understand that the secret to success is not to compete at all. By concentrating on a specific segment of your market, you can cut down competition and establish trust with motivated consumers who are interested in what you want to provide. Here are some tips to help you identify your real estate niche:

Narrow Your Audience

Many brokers and agents pull back at the opportunity cost of committing to their real estate niche. They fear that by minimizing their audience, they are missing on a lot of valuable business. However, it is important to consider the level of quality and competition for that business.

Think of SEO as an analogy. When selecting search keywords to target with your website, general terms like "Los Angeles homes" are hard to rank for as a small or medium-sized business. Probably, many of the consumers typing these terms into Google aren't prepared to purchase a home or speak to an agent, which leads to the question: why compete with them in the first place?

Instead, the correct keyword strategy is developed on winnable terms that show high purchase intent. Similarly, when looking for an audience to establish your real estate niche, concentrate on a smaller but highly motivated group of consumers who will generate better results.

Get Deeper

Getting a potential audience in your market is the first step in building a real estate niche. The most important thing is how you take advantage of it-and that method may not be so general. Take a second look, and you see opportunities that you did not know existed.

If you work in a place with an aging population, for example, senior living communities may appear like a clear channel to success. But go deeper, and you will realize a host of other niches that benefit from the same group.

Be Authentic

You could be tempted to search for a real estate niched depending on its economic upside-but if your heart isn't invested, your audience will not bite. Instead, begin by asking important questions concerning your passions and strengths. What are you good at? Where, how, and with whom do you spend your off-hours? Spend some time in the afternoon to brainstorm, then ask your spouse, friends, and children what they find most exciting about you. Put everything on paper, even when it looks stupid or unrelated to real estate.

Become Hyperlocal

Experts have been discussing for years the value of going "hyperlocal" with your real estate marketing. However, going hyperlocal doesn't imply going after one city or zip code. In fact, you might attain better results by focusing on something smaller. This can be a planned community, a neighborhood, or even one or two streets.

Create Your Own

If you find it difficult to identify a suitable real estate niche, it could be because it has not been invented yet. So why not invent yours, and be the first one.

Best Niches for Real Estate Investing and How to Select Yours

Now that you have some knowledge of selecting real estate niches, let us look at some of the niches in real estate that you can try out.

Niches pay a lot. Just imagine the experts who make the most money like dentists, technicians, contractors, and engineers. Real estate investing niches are not different. They work the same way. The more you focus on a niche, the better you grow financially.

So let's get started.

Niches vs. Strategies

When you first get started in real estate investing, you will have to make two big decisions:

1. Your strategy for real estate investing
2. Your real estate investment niche

Real Estate Investing Strategy

Real estate investing is like climbing a mountain. You as the courageous mountain climber.

The highest point of the mountain is your financial and life goals. And there are multiple milestones along the way.

Strategies are plans you create to help you climb the mountain. These are the routes that will lead you to the peak in the fastest and safest ways.

This section will discuss real estate investment strategies that you can choose.

The strategies are divided into:

- Passive strategies
- Wealth building strategies
- Business strategies
- Debt strategies
- Starter strategies

Business Strategies

These are strategies that produce income and replace your job. But you need to be ready to invest extra time and effort to make them work.

Fix-and-flop

In this strategy, you need to look for properties that need improvement, repairs, and then reselling them at a higher price after making repairs. You can use this strategy as a beginner investor to pay the bills and make some cash savings for future investments. It is not easy, but you will stand a good chance to make some good chunk of money.

Wholesaling

This is the process of looking for better deals on investment properties and reselling them quickly for a small markup. The key part of this business is that you need to be good at marketing and negotiating to land those attractive deals.

If you are good at marketing, you will enjoy wholesaling. However, if the idea of sales makes you sad, then you should look for another strategy.

Starter strategies

These are the safest ways to get started in real estate investing. As a beginner investor, these strategies will work well with you.

Live-in-then-rent

In this strategy, a person lives in a house that later one will become a rental. In other words, the house is your home and an investment.

Live-in-flip

In this strategy, you purchase and move into a home, improve it, and wait for around two years, and resell it again.

Wealth-Building Strategies

The highlight of this strategy is to convert a small nest egg into an on amount of wealth. Real estate investing is ideal for this purpose.

Short-term buy-and-hold

This method requires purchasing and holding rental properties for a short period of time, maybe 1–5 years. Usually, the aim of this strategy is to add value by remodeling.

This strategy is perfect for multi-unit apartment projects. It further works well for rentals in high-value locations.

Long-term buy and hold rentals

This is the method of owning a real estate with the aim of retaining it for a long time. The pros of this slow and steady method include rental income, tax protection from depreciation costs, and price appreciation.

Rental debt snowball plan

This is another great strategy to build wealth, minimize risk, and establish a continuous income stream from rental properties. It involves collecting all the cash flow from your current rentals and any other sources and directing that cash flow to clear mortgage debt at a time.

All-cash rental plan

This method resembles the previous one because it snowballs rental income for development. However, rather than use mortgages, you simply save up cash and purchase a rental property without any debt.

Debt Strategies

This technique subjects you to the profitable role of lender rather than the owner of the real estate.

Hard money lending

This is a strategy of creating short-term loans to real estate investors who purchase rentals or fix-and-flip properties. Normally, the loans require high-interest rates and lower loan to value ratios.

Although the method can be profitable, it also has big risks. If you have to return the properties at foreclosure, you need to ensure that you are protected.

Discounted note investing

This strategy involves buying notes at a discount to the note's full value. As a result of this margin of safety, you can generate large returns and decrease your risk.

Passive Income Strategies

Syndications and crowdfunding

Syndication refers to contributing your money with other investors to purchase real estate or generate loans. It is a means to invest in any of the other methods discussed above without compiling the deals yourself. You invest your cash with syndicators who discover and control deals for you.

Crowdfunding is a new type of syndication where deal opportunities are promoted through online platforms such as Peer Street.

Real estate investment trusts

These are similar to a mutual fund. But rather than allow you to own a piece of many stocks, REITS facilitates ownership of multiple commercial, income-generating properties.

Unlike most of the other investment strategies, this is a truly passive method.

Now that you are familiar with different real estate strategies. Let us switch back to niches.

Real estate niches can be categorized into:

1. Property niches
2. End-user niches

3. Location niches
4. Seller niches

Property Niches

The simplest way to specialize in real estate investing is by property types. Here are the most popular types of investment property.

Single-family houses

Single-family houses exist on their own. Since houses are still popular, single-family houses are one of the best fit for these niches.

However, there are specific high-priced markets that may fail to work financially for house rentals. But don't make an assumption that this is always the case. Do an in-depth search in working-class neighborhoods, and neighborhoods located outside the popular areas. Prices in these places are more affordable.

Small apartment buildings

These buildings are always too small for the big national apartment investors to destroy. However, they are too big for the small, mom-and-pop kind of investors. As a result, they represent an interesting niche for investors ready to pursue them. Financing for these normally arises from commercial lenders such as local banks.

Large apartment buildings

These are buildings that contain over 100 units. There are many advantages to large apartment buildings. For example, the larger the building, the higher the economies of scale exist. This means you get income from many units to pay for the single roof, one property manager, and so forth. You also have the advantage of multiple cash from many units. Since the costs of building these properties are higher, investors normally finance the properties with a mix of commercial loans and capital from partnerships. REITs and other syndications do concentrate on this property type.

Townhomes and condos

Condos and townhomes refer to individual units that belong to a larger complex of units. Since condos are affordable to create, they could be the only affordable investment property present in high priced markets. Like all niches, you need to master the potential pitfalls of condo and townhouse investing. Specifically, with condos, you need to conduct a degree of due diligence on the condo association to master its regulations and meet its financial health.

Mobile homes on land

These have been established in a factory and transported to a piece of land. The manufacturer can build and transport them at a lower cost than the price of a home built on site. For that reason, investors can make higher cash flow from these types of rentals.

Mobile home parks

Mobile home parks consist of multiple single wide mobile homes. Sometimes, the investors own the land and the houses, or the park owner leases spaces to individual owners of homes. This niche differs from small parks with different homes to big parks with hundreds of homes.

This can be a profitable niche with high cash on cash returns. However, the demand for management is always higher for these properties. A strong business system and a great team are a must.

Land

Real estate does not feature the buildings and improvement done on properties alone—it is also the land underneath. Most investors focus on land investing, and there are smaller niches within this big niche. The smaller niche comprises of land development, land leases, timber, and more.

Private partnership

This niche does not fall under the property type, but it is a way for a small or large group of people to invest together. The shared ownership could include various property niches. As opposed to public REITS, syndications are organized between private parties.

Seller Niches

Rather than focus on one type of property, you can select a niche depending on the source of your property purchase.

Seller niches reflect instances in life that make people want to sell.

Property Seller Niches

1. Short sales

Once property owners are behind their mortgage payments, the lender opens a legal action to repossess the property. The interval between the payments falling behind and the actual foreclosure auction is known as pre-foreclosure. This is a profitable niche because the property owner is motivated to sell instead of face the challenge, risk, and embarrassment of foreclosure.

Sometimes, the lender may agree to a specific short sale, which means they will accept less than the complete balance owed on the existing mortgage short sales. Also, short sales work if the property state is bad enough to limit the current market value below the loan balance.

2. Foreclosure auctions

While the process is different in every province or state, a foreclosure finishes with an auction where a judge legally provides the property for sale. The public can submit bids at this auction, but the price is determined by the lender to make sure it covers its loan and expenses. If no one in the public bids high enough, the lender then owns it. Certain investors focus on foreclosure auctions and buy incredible deals. However, there are many legal, property pitfalls, and title to watch out for, so you need to do your homework and get professional help.

3. Bank-owned

This niche features properties owned by banks after a foreclosure auction. In general, the bank makes a profit from interest on loans and not from real estate. So they will always list the properties at aggressive prices to sell them quickly.

You will always find these properties through special REO listing agents and on the MLS. Even though there are bank-owned properties, the strength of the niche repeats depending on the number of properties banks have in inventory. You may also need to have a clear plan to organize REO properties so that you can grab an opportunity quickly when it comes up.

4. Bankruptcy

This is a legal process for businesses or individuals with financial challenges. This helps them eliminate their obligations using the security of a federal bankruptcy court. It is a real estate investment niche because businesses or people trapped in bankruptcy need to sell their properties. Normally, you can purchase bankruptcy properties at very affordable prices.

5. Estates/probate

People are born, as some die. That is the cycle of life. Now, some of the people who die own real estate, and the heirs must decide what they want to do with it. In most cases, the heirs choose to liquidate the property rather than keep it. This creates a way for investors because the heirs could be long-distance, and the property may need some improvements to optimize its value. Proving the option to buy real estate from heirs can be a profitable niche.

6. Water damage or fire

Destruction from water is a traumatic event. Even making an assumption that no one has been hurt—still, the reconstruction, insurance claims, and clean-up can be difficult for the property owner. If the owner had not insured the property, the situation worsens. They might be forced to sell at a drastic discount because no one can move into the property. However, with insurance, some people decide not to rebuild and only sell the property. In either way, a real estate investor who understands how to solve these challenges can build an interesting and profitable niche.

7. Code violations

Most municipalities and towns have rules that dictate the condition of the building and property. The more proactive towns have members employed to cite to owners who fail to fix these problems. Like all citations, code violations should be public record. You, as an investor, can determine which properties have problems, and then you can try to purchase the property. This is a market where you generate profit while solving a problem for the owner, the neighbors, the town members, and many more.

8. Divorce

Divorce is another market type. A divorce may lead to property liquidation. Some real estate investors concentrate on buying properties from people who want to sell quickly without the hassle of displaying it on the open market.

9. Tax delinquencies

The major source of revenue for most local governments. When property owners fail to pay their taxes, the local authorities don't get their money. To solve this challenge, the local government collects taxes using delinquent tax processes.

End-User Niches

End-users refer to customers who support or push real estate investing. They are buyers and tenants who stay in investment properties. Therefore, it is realistic to focus on a niche that helps specific groups of customers.

1. Long-term rentals

This involves buying rentals that interest quality tenants, who stay for years. The biggest rental cost happens during turnovers between tenants. Therefore, if you can establish a niche of long-term rentals, you will reduce your expenses, and save yourself from the hassle, and create enough wealth in the long run.

There is no single property type that matches this category. It will rely on your location.

2. Short-term rentals or Airbnb

The popularity of short-term rentals increased because of the Airbnb website. This niche offers solutions to challenges between hotels and long-term rentals. If a person wants to stay in a place for a few days or even a month, Airbnb allows them to remain in a home setting instead of going to spend time in a cramped hotel.

As an investor, Airbnb will allow you to rent your property or home, or any other creative residence. Short-term rentals may record higher rental rates compared to long term rental. But the drawback is that there is a lot more work to do before you attain this rent.

3. Student rentals

In this niche, you concentrate on investing in college towns or sections of bigger cities where university students stay. This niche has both positives and negatives.

The positive side is that enrollment is always continuous in most universities. This generates a continuous stream of tenants for your properties, and most tenants are creditworthy—therefore, payment problems are scarce. On the other hand, tenants move all the time, so there are more turnover and associated costs. The business is also more management intensive compared to long-term rentals because the tenants are not self-reliant.

4. Government help

One of the programs supported by local and federal governments include housing rent subsidies. These subsidies offer qualified tenants vouchers that can be used to clear section or part of all rent at privately owned rental properties. This benefits rental owners because the government will pay its bills. Based on the location, you can receive a higher rent price compared to renting without vouchers.

Tenants also like to stay longer because other attractive properties ready to accept vouchers are not easy to identify. One of the major challenges of subsidized rentals is handling the paperwork, annual inspections, and bureaucracy.

5. Rent-to-own seller financing

This niche converts renters into homeowners. There are different variations of this particular niche, and some are less than ethical when tenant buyers are taken advantage of. However, when done right, this can be an amazing way to sell your investment property with the least expenses while helping a renter who wishes to become a homeowner.

In some situations, the tenant cashes you out with a new loan. But you can submit seller financing, accept a down payment, and gather principal and interest payments into the future.

The paperwork and legal requirements of this niche are a bit challenging. And that's is the biggest problem. Before you apply a lease option or even seller financing, you need to consult with a local attorney experienced with these types of contracts.

Location

City or town

Towns and cities have important features for real estate investing. Not all towns are the same—some are better **than others.**

Amenities, schools district, and neighborhoods

In every town, specific locations will be more common than others. Parks, greenways, school district, commercial centers, and other amenities can make locations popular. Or in some situations, undesirable features like traffic, noise can make a place less popular. The only way to find out is to get on the street and become a customer.

The secret to selecting your niche is to remain flexible. Be ready to experiment. Be willing to adjust and get started.

You will not find the perfect niche right away, but the process of narrowing down will help you discover your best niche.

CHAPTER 6:

Finding a Motivated Seller

So far, you need to know how to determine the correct value of a property by using the comps you get from a real estate professional. You have now started creating your power team and are now anxious to strike a deal. You are ready to start making cash.

We discussed how you make your money when you purchase a property and the importance of making the right purchase. The correct buying means that you acquire a great deal to optimize your profit on the backend.

In general, you are going to realize that what creates a better deal is finding a motivated or flexible seller. In fact, identifying motivated sellers and helping them with their challenges is the key to great deals.

Who Is a Motivated Seller?

Motivated sellers refer to real estate owners who have to sell for one reason or another. There are different factors that affect their ambition to sell, and these factors are classified into three major categories: the property itself, personal hardships, and economic challenges.

What type of personal hardships might cause a homeowner to become a motivated seller? First, a homeowner experiencing health problems may have to sell the house. Or maybe the owner lands a job outside the state, and the house remains vacant. As time goes, the owner will become more lenient on the price or terms. Maybe the seller has lost the job, and the house is about to go into foreclosure. Or maybe divorce is forcing the sale. Or maybe the owner died, and the house has to be sold to settle the estate and pay the heirs. Or a failed partnership, leading to the sell.

The condition of the property may trigger a need to sell too. Maybe the owner doesn't have enough money to repair it. Sometimes, a property may have a balloon payment due, and the owner is unable to refinance it because the property isn't in the right state to get a loan. Or you might come across a tired landlord with a home that was damaged by the tenants.

Economic challenges can generate a need to sell too. But keep in mind some economic problems you may face can be caused by a change in the overall economy, not just in the economics of the homeowner. For instance, a business that supports the growth of a town, and suddenly goes out of business will have an effect on real estate in the location. Be careful. You may come across phenomenal deals, but are they good deals if you cannot sell the home or rent the house?

How Do We Look for Them?

No matter the factors that trigger the need to sell, the fact is that there are many motivated sellers out there and many methods to find them. By doing so, you can be lucky to strike a great deal.

This chapter will provide you with tips to locate flexible sellers in your place.

Teaming Up with Real Estate Experts

We discussed the significance of having a good real estate agent. While it may take time to find the right one, a real estate expert will help you find motivated sellers. You may have to try out different from them first before you find the best agent for you, but that is fine. Once you find a few agents who have the experience and ability to identify deals, and who will work hard for you, soon you will be receiving numerous phone calls and emails in your inbox.

Collaborating with a real estate agent is often the best way to identify good deals and motivated sellers, especially when you first start out with real estate investing. Search for the ones who know how to be creative and who specialized in working with investors.

How to Work with More Than One Agent

Many investors have more than one agent they work with because it can be very useful to have different agents on your real estate team. A listing agent, for instance, can avoid putting the property on MLS for some days so that an investor has minimal competition for his or her offer. When you collaborate with an agent that has packet listings, they might give you priority at making an offer on a property before they list it on the MLS.

Another type of real estate expert you may enjoy to work with is a foreclosure expert. There are banks that work specifically with specific agents in listing their foreclosures. While not every foreclosure is a deal, some are good to check out.

Another type of real estate expert that you may want to collaborate with is a "hoop jumper"-an agent who is aggressive and work hard for you as a buyer. They attach the keywords into the MLS and retrieve comps for you.

Regardless of how many agents you work with, you need to remember one thing in mind: always be loyal. If you get information from one agent and then buy from another agent, you cannot expect the first agent to continue searching for properties for you. Real estate agents need to be paid something. Always purchase from the one who sends you information first. Be loyal to that agent and aim to create a win-win scenario.

Also, some investors attempt to go around the agent so that they don't pay any fees. But this is not good business. You need to pay something the agent who drives good leads and not try to eat their commission.

Because you will be working with more than one agent, you need to be aware that it may be an issue to an agent that he or she will send you information about a property, only for you to go directly to the homeowner or work with a different agent.

To eliminate such cases, you can suggest signing a Buyer's Agreement. Within the agreement, you agree that you will work with only this agent on a given property he sends you information for a specific period of time. This contract will protect the agent and makes him work hard to search for deals for you.

Using Keywords

The real estate industry can include keywords into the remark section of the MLS to target some interesting properties that fulfill a certain requirement. For example, the real estate agent can include the word "motivated," and the computer will show a listing of every property that contains the word "motivated."

Expired Listings

Once you have a nice relationship with an agent, you can request him or her to retrieve the expired listings and show you. Sometimes, the MLS system can allow your agent to search for properties that are free and clear.

Designing a Flyer to Attract Aggressive Agents

If you want to catch the attention of agents who may already have motivated sellers or who are aware of interesting properties, you may want to consider running an ad or even send a flyer to all the real estate offices within your field of interest.

For Sale by Owner Signs

By now, you might be already taking a different path to work every day. You need to pay attention to any for sale by owner signs. That is because some of these properties may not have been printed in the newspaper, and the only method to learn about them is to read the signs. Poorly advertised FSBO houses are a great source of leads. Write down the telephone number and call the owner. Even much better, open your car door, and knock on the gate.

Looking for Vacant or Boarded Houses

Anytime that you are in a car, you need to be on the lookout for vacant houses, houses for rent, distressed properties, and FSBOs. Drive around your target area regularly and search for these properties. Owners of vacant or distressed properties can be distressed sellers.

Write down the addresses of any vacant homes you come across. You can search for the owner's name at the courthouse. If you aren't in a hurry, stop the car, step out and knock on neighbors' doors. They could be aware of where the owner moved to, or they may have the contact details of the owner.

Many neighbors discover that a vacant house is reducing the value of their home, and they will be ready to assist you in finding the owner. If they know how to get the owner, but are scared to give you this information, you can always leave them with your business card and tell them to notify the owner that you could be interested in buying the home.

Leave a few flyers at the vacant house. The owner or a family member may come across it while checking the house.

Getting Owners of Vacant Houses

- Search for the owner's name on the tax rolls, or computerized services. Or you can check online.

- Confirm with the neighbors on both sided of the house and find out whether they know how to reach the owners or where they have moved.

- Send two letters, one to the address of the vacant house, and the other one to the address with the following words "Address Service Requested-Do Not Forward" on the envelope.

- Look at the phone book or call details to determine whether a new number has been released to the owner or if they have a new address.

If you have a separate mailing address for the owner, but it is not listed in the phone book, look at the reverse directory, which is found in the reference section of your public library. The directory begins with addresses first, letting you search for the owner's name when the only information you have is their address. Sometimes, the owner might be living with relatives with separate last name and reverse directories can allow you find them.

- Involve a private investigator to instruct them to perform a skip trace to identify the owner. Try to negotiate with them that they should find the information you are searching for, or there is a fee.

Auctions

Search in the Yellow Pages and in newspaper advertisements for auctioneers. Call each auctioneer you come across and ask them if they can auction real estate. If they accept, request to be included on their mailing list. If you see an auction for real estate property being marketed or if you get a notice from an auctioneer, call and get the address of the property. Drive near the house. If you like the house, submit an offer for them to present before the auction happens.

Absolute auctions

An absolute auction means they will accept whatever it is bid. Typically, banks have 14 months to sell a Real Estate Owned property. If by this time it is not sold, they have to unload the property quickly. You normally have to register to be able to bid. Register and acquire a bidder's card.

Foreclosure auctions

Visit a foreclosure auction. If you plan to purchase at this auction, make sure you do your research well. You will also need cash. There will be stiff competition. This is also a great place to meet other investors to connect with. Go there with the intention to network with other investors you can purchase from or quick-turn properties too.

FDIC, VA, IRS, and Many More

In certain parts of the country, the department of housing and VA foreclosure properties are great deals. To identify foreclosure properties offered by the department of housing, you can visit the HUD website.

Keep in mind this, never bid an owner-occupied list unless you want to live in the property. If you have no plans to live in the property, you need to wait until it shows up on the list that it is open to all bidders.

Garage Sales

When you see a garage or a yard sale, step out of your car and speak to the owners. Keep in mind what most people do before they list their house for sale. They de-junk. Someone with a garage sale may be prepared to sell his or her home. But even if they are not ready to sell, they may know of someone else who is. You will always find them to be friendly and talkative. Talk to them about the neighborhood. Do they know the kind of houses to sell for? Do they know of anyone planning to sell? Leave them your business card.

Courthouse Records

The courthouse is a great source for researching and finding motivated sellers. Find out where the records are stored in your courthouse. Sometimes, you may be moving to different places of the courthouse depending on what you are researching. Search for foreclosures.

A foreclosure will inevitably spark motivation. As said before, foreclosure doesn't always mean a great deal, but certain foreclosure properties are great deals. When handling a foreclosure, there are four timeframes that offer the best opportunities.

Private Noteholders

Most private noteholders are investors. They might own different properties, or they may be hard money lenders. In general, not all private noteholders are investors. However, if you notice a private holder with different notes, then you have actually found an investor. A private note holder can become a very motivated seller if they have to foreclose a property they hold.

Divorce Cases

Divorce is a major cause of foreclosure. Even when a couple does not lose their home to foreclosure, divorce can cause big financial hardship and motivate the couple to sell. You need to have complete disclosure with both sellers signing any agreement.

Houses with Tax Liens

When a homeowner experiences problem paying their taxes, it is normally a sign they are having financial challenges. In most cases, there is a lot of equity in the home, and you may help solve their challenges and create a win-win situation.

Out-of-State Owners

If you can identify out-of-state owners, you may discover a more flexible seller. It can be a big problem to manage a property from far. Or sometimes the owner has to move quickly and now the house is sitting empty. Sometimes, a title company will have the permission to retrieve this information for you from the county records.

Bird Dogs

These are referrals who behave act as your ears and eyes searching for leads on your behalf. For the hard work they do, you pay them finder's fee.

Who can be your prospective bird dogs? Think of the individuals who stay in the neighborhoods daily, such as the mail carrier and cable installer. These people are constantly visiting your prime target areas. You can also speak to garbage collectors, lawn service workers, code enforcement officers, newspaper delivery, and many more.

Signs

A fluorescent yellow sign featuring black writing catches the attention of people. Make it simple such that it is easy to read from a distance, and highlight your contact details. Post your signs wherever you are allowed in your city. For example:

- Movie theaters
- Grocery store carts
- Bus stop benches
- Utility posts
- Community billboards
- Main intersections

Bulletin Boards

Post flyers anywhere you see bulletin boards like grocery stores, restaurants, a city center, and mail centers.

Each time you enter a business place, confirm whether they provide a community bulletin board where you can submit your information.

Flyers

Design a simple and attractive flyer. Drop it door to door in the neighborhoods where you want to purchase.

You can employ students or individuals from your local labor board to drop the flyers.

Handouts

You can distribute handouts anywhere that it is allowed. You could be able to spread the handouts at some school or local events.

Driving for Dollars

As you drive by houses looking for vacant houses, do you have your signs in the back of your car along with a staple gun and tape? Every time you notice a vacant house, not only should you write down the address, but you need to get out of the car and put a sign on the vacant house. Make sure the signs are large enough to be read from the street. You are not only looking for the owner, but you also want to find motivated sellers who may happen to see the sign and call you.

Cooperative Advertising

Have you ever received a main that features ads for different companies in a single envelope? Everyone contributes to the production costs, minimizing your own cost. Ensure the message is simple. The mailing company may have professionals who can help you design a beautiful ad.

Get in touch with different credit unions or banks. Speak to the branch manager and notify them that you are involved in sending emails and request them to join you.

Direct Mail

Ensure that once you mail people in your target area, you repeat the process. It may take up to four mailings for most people to respond. If you want to target a particular area, you can gather a list of owners and addresses from your title company. Some people will apply a reverse address book.

Restrooms

In certain public restrooms, low-cost advertising is provided on the back of the stall doors.

CHAPTER 7:

Real Estate Business Plan

There is no successful business that is established without proper planning. A plan serves as the guide for the development of the structure—without which the building just won't be there. Hence, carefully creating your real estate business plan is a vital part of your journey.

This chapter will look at the options you have in creating that plan and will get you ready for your entrance and long-term success in real estate investing.

Your success in the real estate niche doesn't happen in a second, and it doesn't come without the right planning. Therefore, establishing a real estate investing business plan is a process that every new property investor has to make. In this chapter, you will learn the steps you need to take to get started, what resources are required, what needs to be done, and what you should expect. For that reason, a great plan acts like a roadmap that provides you directions and keeps you on track to succeed.

Goals

The first part of a great business plan for a real estate investor is writing down what you want to achieve from this business. The goals that you set should be SMART. For example, if you want to earn $3,000 a month in rental income, or fix-and-flip one investment property a month, or to purchase and rent two investment properties every year. By having a detailed picture of where you want to reach in the future as a real estate investor, you will have a better understanding of the investment decisions that you need to make to attain that goal.

Don't forget that every goal should have a time frame. Similarly, it is a great idea to think ahead in terms of short-term and long-term goals and apply them in your real estate investing business plan. Also, avoid subjective goals like to retire early, to get rich selling real estate, or to be the best. If your future goals are blurry, you will never realize when or how you will achieve them.

Investment Strategy

Now that you understand why you are investing in the business and what you want to get, the next part of the real estate investing business plan contains your strategy to achieve those goals. This means, how are you going to convert an investment property into profits? Do you want to purchase –and hold real estate, fix-and-flip properties, invest in short-term investment, or different investment strategies?

The correct answer depends on:

Type of Investment Property

You need to be specific. The real estate industry has many forms of investment properties. There are vacation rentals, single-family homes, townhomes, etc.

Real Estate Market

Property investors need to research their market to find out whether it's in the best location or not.

Financial Plan

Financing a real estate investment is a major worry for first-time property investors. To check a good financing plan, you need to confirm where you stand financially today. Determine the amount of cash that you have. Do you have equity that you can take advantage of? You might be capable of purchasing your first investment property with cash, or you need to look for other alternative financing options. Your real estate investing business plan should define the precise model of financing.

Understanding how you will complete the purchase is going to prevent you from changing your original goals and plans. Also, when you establish a financial plan, it is important to include expenses such as repairs, property management, interest rates, and taxes. Additionally, ensure you update your financials as your business keeps growing.

Marketing Plan

Owning a rental property is a good thing, but what is the point if prospective buyers cannot identify it? To have a powerful marketing strategy, property investors first require to focus on a particular audience. For instance, do you plan to rent out to millennial tenants or baby boomers?

The next thing is to highlight something special about your rental property and differentiate it from others. Additionally, ensure your marketing plan attracts and reaches your target audience. Nowadays, millennials depend on technology to search for their next property. Therefore, you must have social media marketing.

Timeframe

This is the time you will take to achieve your goals. You need to be realistic when setting this time, but you should not be scared to reach.

Flexibility

If you aren't getting enough deals, you can change your strategy. Many first-time investors are excited to purchase the first deal that comes their way. However, if you have a well-defined strategy, you can easily reject properties that are not a good deal.

Exit and Backup Plans

Having different and clearly defined strategies is the most critical part of your business plan, particularly for new investors. How are you going to close the deal? What are your backup plans? This needs to be elaborate.

The Bottom Line

Business plans and road maps are guides and not rules. A business plan is supposed to direct you and inspire you to implement it. When you have a good business plan, executing the plan and visualizing the results becomes easy.

Successful property investors look at their investment as a business, and that is why they have a real estate investing business plan.

Remember that a business plan is not a document that you complete once and never take a look at it again. A real estate investor should regularly check and update his/her business plan while his or her investment portfolio grows, and new information arises.

CHAPTER 8:

Winning Financing

Now, you know how to make your money in real estate when you purchase and, therefore, the significance you need to consider making the right purchase. Always remember never to pay too much money for the property. When you make the right purchase, you ensure you get the correct deal. As you already know, the secret to landing a great deal is finding a motivated seller. However, to become successful in real estate investing, you need to understand not only how to search for motivated sellers and the best deals but also how to find the cash for those deals.

Financing is an important element in real estate because it can make or break the deal. So you have perhaps been asking the common questions where many beginner investors ask, "Where can I get the money to finance the deals?"

Well, to finance your deals, you can involve traditional lenders such as mortgage companies and banks. However, if you don't have the best credit or you have a high debt-to-income ratio, you may have to search for alternative sources of money. This chapter will explore creative financing options available to you, so regardless of your situation, you will have the tools you need to close the deal.

Become Creative

The more creative you become as you finance your deal, the higher the chances of success. A critical aspect of creative real estate investing is how better you solve the problems of your sellers. Motivated sellers have a problem, and as you solve this problem, you create a win-win situation.

You can generate a lot of money helping others solve their challenges. And as you learn the different approaches and strategies, you will understand the terms and can be important than the price of an equity.

You may have heard from people that there is no such thing as no money down deal. This can discourage you, particularly if you hear this from a professional in the industry.

You may even hear some investors say that you need to have money to purchase real estate. But consider this: These people haven't used any creative financing channel or no money down approaches, so they do not know how you can own property without any money. That said, even though a lot of investors have purchased real estate properties without any money, creative channels of finances do not always mean no money.

Overall, it refers to not using any of your own money. But instead, you want to use OPM. Applying different strategies and methods will provide you with endless means to fund your deals.

Establishing successful no money down transaction arises from understanding the relevant details that will fulfill the needs of the seller.

Working with Mortgage Brokers

As you start to create your real estate team, you will notice a good mortgage broker is required to get financing for every transaction. You're looking for a creative broker who collaborates with investors often and has multiple financing programs available. Mortgage brokers are more creative than bankers because they have different sources of funds and different loan programs at their hands. Sometimes, you may discover a small hometown bank will be anxious to help you in investing. Some of these hometown banks give portfolio loans. Once a lender sells a loan, there are special rules they have to follow. If you have a good relationship with your banker and they do portfolio loans, they can be more lenient. Otherwise, you will definitely discover other creative financing requiring a mortgage broker.

Some mortgage brokers have access to private funds that need no qualification by the borrower.

Equity in the house is their main concern. It is not the cost of the money that is important, but the availability that matters. You require a mortgage broker anytime you are going to handle short-term money unless you plan to create relationships with your own private lenders. In general, the money these mortgage brokers will acquire for you comes from private individuals. The only consideration for one of these private loans is the Loan-to-Value ratio.

This short-term cash is important to us as investors because you can get a loan on the value of the house, and not what you paid for it.

In this case, if you buy right, you can borrow the cash to both buy the property and cover the costs to fix it up. You only factor these expenses into the cost of the loan. Additionally, private investors are only focused on LTV ratio and the security of the investment.

In general, private money is referred to as "hard money," and sometimes they are called hard money lenders. A hard money lender will lend at a low LTV, about 60-75% of the after-repair value (ARV).

Contacting Mortgage Brokers

To get in touch with mortgage brokers, find out whether you can get a referral from a real estate agent or a different real estate investor. Or look in your phonebook or newspaper and call those who appear creative.

You don't need to set an appointment and meet with the broker; you only need to call. It requires some time from your busy schedule to go and meet with a broker only to realize that she or he cannot help you, so you need to start by making a call.

When you call a mortgage broker, you may find someone who is rude, and someone you are not comfortable working with. Politely thank you very much and hang up.

When you speak with several brokers, some will answer you rudely, but a good number of them will be ready to help you.

However, when calling bankers or mortgage brokers, you should never give them your social security number. Every time they do a credit check, it reduces your score. Before you let the broker check your credit, you will want to ensure that they can help you.

If you happen to know your score, tell them what it is. But don't reveal your Social Security Number until you are sure this is the broker you want to collaborate with.

Once you finalize on the broker you want to work with, then it fine to allow them to run your credit and make a loan application so that you can know the amount of loan you qualify to get.

Questions to Ask Mortgage Brokers

1. What is the highest you can lend a non-owner occupied property? What is the least amount?

2. What is the highest percentage you will lend an owner-occupied property? What is the highest for investor loans?

3. Is that amount based on the appraised value? In most cases, they will say the purchase price.

4. Do you permit the seller to take back a note?

5. Do you allow piggybacks? This is where the broker uses either the same lender, but two loans or two different lenders. Typically, it is 80% in the 1st mortgage and a 20% in the second mortgage. That is 100% financing. The 20% is generally higher—it can be as much as 10% interest.

6. Do you have any creative financing or hard money? If they say they do, find out the kind of creative financing they have. Can they register you without any money? Do they have

access to most of the hard money and constantly work with private investors? Also, find out about the terms of the private investors as they can differ from lender to lender.

7. Do you have equity lenders? Equity lenders tend to give a low LTV, normally between 60-70% of the appraised value. In general, they are not as expensive as a hard money lender. The loan is always a short-term loan of 1-2 years, and there is a prepayment penalty on loan.

8. Do you provide any loans for fixing up the property? Sometimes, they have rehab loans to correct the property or construction loans where they lend you the money to purchase the property and rehab it.

9. Do you have any non-conforming loans, given the strict lending guidelines?

Here are examples of non-conforming loans:

- **Stated income Loans -** You doesn't need to prove how much money you earn. It initially started for business owners who take a huge deduction.

- **No ratio loans** - This does not have a debt-to-income ratio. They will confirm employment and assets, but not your income. If you are self-employed, they need to review a two-year business license or a verification from a CPA of two years' employment.

- **NINA** - This does not have income or asset verification. They will review your credit and verify you have a job. They will not verify where you are getting your down payment. It can arise from a third party. They don't care where the money comes from.

- **NO DOC** - This does not have documentation. This loan only requires verification of where you have lived for the last two years—no assets, no employment, and no income. These loans have a higher interest compared to conforming loans, but provide more versatility to an investor.

10. Is the loan based on the property itself or you look at my income? If you are purchasing a property, they will compute 75% of the income. As long as your mortgage, insurance, taxes are less than 75%; you should not have a lot of problems qualifying for a loan.

11. Up to how many units can you lend? Four are said to be residential. Five or more than five are said to be commercial. Commercial loans are different from residential loans.

12. What is the rate of interest? This will change from day to day, but it is important to have a ballpark number.

13. What type of fees do you charge? When they discuss points, remember that one point is equivalent to one percent of the loan.

14. Do you permit the seller to pay the closing costs? How much does closing costs normally run? They will often allow the seller to pay 3% of the purchase price in closing costs.

15. Do you support some form of seller concession, such as a repair or decorating allowance? Normally, they will let the seller give a repair that will appear during closing. They always allow a specific percentage.

16. How long do I have to wait to get approval? How fast can you close? You want to make sure you set enough timeframe in your contract. Overall, make your closing date a bit longer than the broker expects it to be.

Seller Financing

Seller financing is a method of buying real estate without depending on the bank.

You can think of it as a loan, even though no money changes hand between the buyer and seller. However, the buyer always makes a deposit, and then the seller receives the rest of the money in installments.

At the basic form, seller financing simply means the seller of the real estate property waits to receive all of the remaining of her sales price. Rather than get the whole amount in cash at closing, the seller carriers part or all of the price using owner financing contracts.

There are different forms of seller financing. For example:

1. A seller has equity in the property.
2. The seller deeds the property to the buyer.
3. The buyer provides the seller with a promissory note.
4. The buyer provides the seller a mortgage to protect the promissory note against the property.

Other terms associated with seller financing include:

- Owner financing
- Bond-for-title
- Rent-to-town
- Contract-for-deed
- Installment sale

- Seller carry-back financing
- Subject to the mortgage

The Pros and Cons of Seller Financing

You know that there are always pros and cons to every method. Seller financing is not an exception.

So, below, you will find the pros and cons of seller financing.

- Easier to qualify - The seller still has to trust you, but in general, it has less paperwork and hassles than a bank loan.

- Lower interest Rate - Especially compared with private financing

- Lower down payment

- Everything is negotiable.

- No personal guarantee - With most loans, you include all your personal assets in case the lender loses money. However, this can be excluded from seller financing contracts so that only the property is security for the debt.

- Faster, and easier closing - You eliminate layers of bureaucracy, repetitive processes, and appraisals.

- Potential discount on the loan balance - Sometimes, the seller may need cash. Therefore, they could be ready to allow you to pay off all or part of the loan at a discount in exchange for a huge sum of money.

- An important relationship for more business

Drawbacks of Seller Financing from the Buyer's Perspective

- **Everything is negotiable**. While this is a pro, it's also a disadvantage in the sense that you need to know what terms to negotiate. There is a learning curve. So you may better consider using a local attorney.

- **Difficult to negotiate.** Seller financing requires that you have the skills to negotiate and stay patient.

- **Problems with heirs.** If the original seller dies, you will engage with the estate and the heir. You have a protected contract, so this should not be a bad thing. But it may require commitment and communication than with a bank loan.

Pros of Seller Financing from the Seller's Perspective

- **Continuous income.** If the type of property was a rental, the seller probably enjoyed the regular income. Seller financing goes on with that income stream without the issue of ownership and management.

- **It is more passive.** Changing from a landlord to a lender is a good progression.

- **Familiar investment.** The seller always owns the property for some time. Thus, owning a mortgage secured by the same property is familiar and can be nice than unfamiliar investments somewhere else.

- **Tax planning.** The IRS considers an installment sale as a means to defer a capital gain on a property sale. This could save on taxes by eliminating a bump up into a higher tax level if the seller had a big profit.

- **Higher price.** By providing terms, the seller usually acquires a higher sales price than if they sold for cash.

- **Estate planning.** What can most estate heirs do with a huge sum of cash?

Drawbacks of Seller Financing from the Seller's Perspective

Disadvantages of seller financing from the perspective of the seller.

- **Trust in the buyer.** Banks approve borrowers for a reason. So, a seller has to look for a way to trust the competence and personality of the buyer so that payments are made and the property does not get old.

- **Inflation**. Any fixed payment investment involves seller financing notes, becomes less valuable as inflation happens.

- **Tax planning**. The long-term landlord seller will likely experience tax on depreciation recapture at the time of sale.

Tips for Seller Financing

- Approach the negotiation slowly, with the objective of helping the seller.

- Concentrate on building trust first before you say unfamiliar terms such as "seller financing."

- Once the seller is receptive, describe the pros and cons of seller financing.

- Create multiple offers, at least one of which is seller financing. You cannot tell the kind of offer they want.

- Use seller financing as a method to purchase property that suits into your general investing strategy.

Type of Owners Who Will Finance Their Properties

The number of people who can sell your property is many. However, sellers ready to carry back the financing is much smaller. So, you need to know first who those people are before you start searching for owner financing properties.

- Savvy investor
- Sister and brother who inherited their childhood property
- An investor who cannot handle the intensive management of a property in a low-rent neighborhood
- Investor ready to retire and travel but wants continuous passive income
- An individual who has inherited a property from his mother

The Bottom Line with Seller Financing

When there is no cash offered as a down payment, the seller might be worried that if the property is destroyed, they could lose money. The property itself may not satisfy the debt. If you give them something extra like your other property, they may be at peace knowing that the extra collateral will provide them with some cushion.

But in most cases, you will find a seller who wants some down payment first. Now, you need to determine the needs of the seller are.

Does the seller need some cash immediately? Or does the seller feel that if you have a vested interest in the property, you will take good care of it and make the monthly payments? This means, is the seller looking for security alone?

If the seller wants cash and a huge down payment, maybe the seller could subordinate his position, letting you acquire the first mortgage with a lender and have the seller hold a second mortgage.

If the seller does not want to hold a lien, then maybe you can offer the seller some more cash and have a lower mortgage.

Due on Sale Clause and Land Trusts

There are occasions where the seller has a mortgage on the property, but they may be willing to collaborate with you. If the mortgage can be assumed and does not demand a buyer to qualify, then you can ignore the mortgage and request the seller to carry a second mortgage for the difference between the buying price and the ignored mortgage.

However, when the mortgage is not assumable, or when qualification by a new buyer is mandatory for an assumption to happen, there will be an acceleration clause within the mortgage that says if the property is sold, the lender has the permission to ask for payment of the remaining principal balance. This is referred to as a "due-on-sale clause."

Wraparound Mortgages

This is an important element in purchasing houses when a property has an existing mortgage. A wrap is a seller carry-back loan that supports financing. It allows the buyer to attain financing without completing the existing loan.

The buyer's mortgage and payments depend on the terms of the wrap and have no connection with the existing financing. The seller maintains the difference between what he or she gets from the buyer and the mortgage payment of the existing financing.

A Land Contract and Agreement for Deed

These terms all mean the same thing: a promise to pay. Until the debt is cleared, the seller retains the title, and the buyer gets an equitable interest in the property.

The buyer doesn't become the titleholder until the contract terms are fulfilled—at this point, the seller deeds the property to the buyer.

A contract sale is stored by an escrow company that has the warranty deed approved by the seller until the buyer completes the terms of the contract.

The advantage of applying land contracts or contract deed is that they can be applied as a means to avoid the due-on-sale clause because the title does not transfer until the terms are completed. Another advantage is there are minimum closing costs required because owner financing is applied.

Other No- or Low-Money Techniques

Ignore the First Mortgage and Let the Seller Carry a Second

One technique is to ignore the first mortgage and let the seller carry a second. Normally, there is a big difference between what you have discussed with the seller as a purchase price and the assumable loan he or she has. This difference can drain your pocket quickly, or make the deal far from attaining. Request the owner to carry a second mortgage for the difference.

The Owner Takes Back a Note

Another approach is to let the owner take back a note for a short period of time, giving you a chance to receive a refinance loan rather than a purchase loan. A refinance is focused on the appraised value and not the buying price; therefore, if you are buying below the appraised value, you can get into the property without any money. It can have an interest in adding up and mortgage payments.

But you need to exercise caution when applying the following technique. Make sure you have a lender who can refinance quickly without seasoning and one who will base that refinance on appraised value even if you haven't owned the property for long.

Split Funding

In this technique, the investor provides a certain portion of the money to close the deal, while the remaining amount is due in a few months. There is no interest paid, and only a single large payment is made.

The terms are negotiable, but gives time for the investor to correct the property and have it sold before the balloon is due. The benefit to the seller is that a distressed property is fixed up, and the seller receives his or her money before the balloon payment is due.

Balloon the Down Payment

Same as split funding except that there is no cash released. But you request the seller to carry the note and wait for the down payment. The period of waiting can be six months or longer.

Pay the Down Payment in Small Amounts

You can request the seller to allow you to complete the down payment in small amounts. The payments can be made over a few months or years. But if you are holding the property for income, you may want to ensure it has cash flow.

Subordination

This is the process of transferring a senior loan to a junior position. It qualifies you to earn a new mortgage, although you already have a seller financing in place. This means subordination happens when the seller accepts to take back a second mortgage and lets you earn a first new mortgage on the property. This method works well with properties having low mortgages.

Sellers may be ready to subordinate because they have a distressed property they cannot sell. Or they may receive a lot of money from you with subordination compared to what they would get if they sold the property "all cash" to another buyer.

Keep in mind that the sales price can sometimes mean a lot to the seller than the cash.

Substitution of Collateral

This is where you take an existing mortgage on a single property and transfer it to another. In other words, you are substitute collateral from one property to another. This can work well for a down payment or can be used to buy the property. Now, you will own it free and clear. Next, you can refinance it, setting aside cash for future investments to clear the loan that was applied on an existing property that you own.

Joint Venture with the Seller

Request the seller to assist you in selling his or her property, and split the profit between you. If there is so much equity, or you can push the appreciation by doing some little repair, both you and the seller can make some good cash. Ensure you sign a contract that states the amount you will split and the terms you have agreed for your security.

Joint Venture with an Investor

Assume you find a good deal, but you don't have enough money. You can involve another investor to be your partner. In the commercial field, an investor will bring other investors.

Partners

If you use partners, then you must have all your numbers calculated, and the whole deal carefully planned. It is a rule of thumb to split the profit equally.

You can find a partner by attending a local real estate investment group.

Note

When you involve a partner, ensure that you get in touch with the attorney. It might not be your desire to form a partnership. Many people have been negatively affected because of partnering.

CHAPTER 9:

The Art of Negotiation

The Psychology of Negotiating

One of the major factors to remember when discussing with others is that you are working with people, many of whom create an emotional connection in the process.

Most of the buyers and sellers that you will interact with are not experts and always find it hard to hide their emotions from the rational elements needed to run a business. After a certain period, people become emotionally connected, which prompts them to act in a certain way they would otherwise not. This is particularly true for sellers.

For instance, a person who has had his property listed for sale for some months may start to worry about whether his property will ever sell. Then, one day, a buyer emerges who shows a genuine interest in the house. The seller starts to think there is hope. The real estate agents hint that an offer may be becoming. The seller becomes eager and excited at the idea that he can sell his house and proceed with his plans.

He wonders about all the things he can do with the cash he will generate from the sale—the new car, clearing some debts, and buying a beautiful gift for his wife.

Just as the buyer is about to submit an offer, she comes across another house that she finds better and purchases it instead. Feelings of despair sets in the seller. All his hopes and dreams collapse, for once again, it looks like he will never sell his house.

While negotiating, remember that at a certain point in the negotiating process, the parties you are working with will become emotionally engaged. Once they become, it is hard for them to change. In their minds, they know that the property is sold and they are already using the cash. As a professional, you need to watch closely for signs sent by another member's facial expressions and body language.

Detailed Knowledge of the Market

To succeed in this particular business, you must have a detailed knowledge of your market. It is hard to negotiate for the correct price without it. You need to understand the property values in your market, better than the people you are doing business with. You can apply your knowledge to make good judgments about the price and terms you are negotiating for. By revealing to the other parties what similar properties are selling for, you provide realistic and logical data that will assist persuade them of your position.

Whether you want to buy single-family houses, vacant lands, or apartment buildings, you cannot manage to overpay for a single property. As an expert real estate investor, you need to be familiar with the market where you are working. Only by having a detailed knowledge of it can you be very successful. Without this critical information, you will soon realize that you cannot survive in the business of purchasing and selling real estate.

The Level of the Seller's Motivation

As a real estate expert, it is important for you to understand why a given seller is selling a property. Being aware of the underlying reasons for the sale can provide you an advantage at the time of negotiation. For example, you want to know whether the seller has lost a job and can no longer manage to make payments, or maybe is just trying to see how much the property is worth in the market. This means you want to understand whether the seller is a motivated seller, and to what degree. The more motivated the seller is, the more likely he or she will be flexible on both terms and price. Although there are many reasons for selling, they usually fall into one or more of the following reasons listed below.

1. Relocation
2. Retirement
3. Investor burnout
4. Investor gains
5. Changes in financial status
6. Life-changing events
7. Tax considerations

The main reason why sellers opt to sell their properties is because of changes in life. Life-changing events such as the birth of a baby, marriage, accident, death, divorce, and many more. These events are referred to as high-degree motivations that cause one or more family members to sell their properties. They require and want to do so fast and are unlikely to hold out for a top dollar. The affected sellers by these situations usually have a very real and immediate need to sell, and hence are more likely to be flexible about both price and terms.

Life-changing events always trigger an urgent need to sell, which exceeds the need to profit from the transaction.

Experiencing a divorce, for instance, always triggers financial difficulty for the family, particularly in a traditional household where the father is the provider, and the mother is the main giver to the children. In this case, all members of the family are affected. Where one big house was enough before, two smaller houses or apartments will be important now.

The other reason why sellers sell their properties directly is associated with changes in their financial status. These changes may also be a high-degree motivator, based on the level of financial change.

The most likely cause of the financial problem is a change in the employment sector. The seller could have been trapped in the current state of downsizing or whatever the current buzzword might be.

The bottom line is that the seller is now unemployed and hence no longer able to meet his or her financial needs. Changes in a seller's financial status may also be a result of a life-changing event.

As you interact with sellers, find out from them the reasons why they are selling. Listen to both what they say and do what they avoid telling you. Sometimes, they can be very direct. Other times, you will need to pay attention and listen for subtle clues about their genuine reason for selling. They might tell you, for instance, that they are retiring but exclude the part that they have already bought a condo that is forcing them to pay twice and really stretching their budget.

Some probing can always reveal the underlying reasons to sell.

Backdoor Exits

These allow you to exit from a purchase contract at different times throughout the entire contract period. You must always take care to make sure that different escape clauses are included in the contract, with at least one of the clauses providing you the right to back out immediately. The correct application of these techniques can supply the shrewd investor with vast bargaining power.

Plan B is a common backdoor exit that many investors use. The type of contingency is restricted only by your imagination.

Concessions

Concessions can be another effective approach to finding just what you want during the time of negotiation. Sellers can be anxious to say yes to everything you ask for. On the flip side, they might instead present an opposing offer to partially decrease the price, pay for the closing expenses, and provide you a credit for repairs, but not to include the appliances.

You can also use concession as a tool for bargaining. For example, you say to the seller that you will agree to X if you agree to Y. An example of this type of bargaining is an agreement to pay the seller's full asking price if he agrees to accept only 5% instead of the 20% originally desired. Another instance is the seller who must have all the cash and is pushing for a quick closing.

You accept her request, but only if she agrees to accept $10, 000 less than the asking price. Concessions are accurately used to get something in your favor connected to the transaction in exchange for something else.

The Red Herring Approach

This technique creates interference that is completely irrelevant to the subject at hand. As an expert investor, you can use this approach to stir a distraction from the main issue you are negotiating.

The Money-Talks Approach

This approach can be an effective negotiation tool to make sure that extra offers are accepted. While the technique is simple in its application, the outcome can be quite powerful. There is a great deal of truth in the phrase "money talks." Here is how it works, once you write your offer to include other negotiation methods discussed earlier, now is the time to submit it to the seller. When submitting your offer, including a large check to show the seller that you are a serious buyer. In general, the check should be written between 5 to 10 percent of the deal value. This will rely on the housing prices in your specific market. A large earnest-money deposit sends a strong and instant signal to the seller that he or she is handling with a buyer who is both capable of compiling a deal.

Finding the best possible price and terms for the purchase of the real estate demands a combination of both art and skill. As an expert negotiator, you need to take care to exercise each of the above steps.

How to Master Real Estate Negotiations

Most real estate agents and clients look at negotiation simply as how they price their listing or their offer to purchase. Maybe they include the idea of a counteroffer in their negotiation toolkit. The reality is that proper negotiation is much more than just the price on a home or earnest deposit.

Negotiation Is Really an Art in Real Estate

Never assume an aggressive posture in ANY of your interactions with real estate agents, sellers, or buyers. Just the opposite, you must be easy to get along with and easy to speak to.

But don't forget that you are there for one reason: to find answers to your real estate needs whether you are purchasing or selling. This means that while you are negotiating the deal, each piece of information that you give to the other side should be carefully released at just the perfect time, spoken in just the right way and meant to change your position in the interaction.

Experience shows that the "art of negotiation" isn't just a simple isolated exchange, but a continuous effort. You need to every step that you take during the whole transaction starting with submittal of an offer to close of escrow as part of this negotiation.

Structure Your Offer for Acceptance

A great buyer's agent will train their clients about the right methods to position themselves and their offer to boost the chances of the seller's acceptance.

This is correct even in a strong buyer's market because if you want to pay the least price for a property, you need to be sure that all the other elements to your offer besides the price are as attractive as possible.

Keep in mind that while the price is crucial to the seller, so are the other elements of the deal. The seller only wants to use the escrow process ONE TIME, so if all the aspects of your offer must say "I can CLOSE," your least-price offer may be preferable to a bigger offer.

The Home Inspection Is a Common Negotiation Tool

Negotiation is critical on the seller side of the transaction. For instance, most buyer-agents will ask their clients to quote huge price reductions from the seller for relatively low repairs that are found during the buyer's home inspection.

A good listing agent should request the seller to do a home inspection before they list the property, and then correct the items identified in the inspection. This method completely excludes the home inspection as a tool for bargaining from the buyer's side of the transaction.

Be Proactive and Not Reactive

During a real estate negotiation, it is better to be proactive instead of reactive. It is vital to stay positive, respond from a position of strength, communicate early, and use empathy. Avoid being negative and reactive, acting from the point of weakness, and not listening to the other party's true interests and needs.

Unfortunately, many people like to speak more than listen during a hot real estate negotiation. This always results in no deal for anyone. Listen carefully to the other party. They are likely to inform you of the easiest route to get the quickest solutions.

Questions Results in Positive Answers and Results

To close a deal, both parties must be flexible and open-minded. Be ready to compromise and change your own mind. When attempting to convince someone else to change their mind, make them question their own statements.

During debates, many people will concentrate on a definitive statement said by the other party, such as "you're wrong" or "the roof is 100% okay with no leaks," unlike questioning their own beliefs. Changing one's mind first starts with changing how we speak to ourselves. Questioning our thoughts then results in a more flexible and open mindset.

Real Estate Negotiation Techniques

To boost your chances of success, use these strategies when negotiating for real estate.

- **Develop a positive attitude.** Keep a smile and allow the other party to feel appreciated. We all want to feel loved and liked. So focus on staying positive.

- **Negotiate physically.** Don't try to negotiate over the phone. Humans tend to react to the body language and tone of the other person than spoken words. When you negotiate through texts or emails, it is not easy to learn the tones and intentions of the other person. Some people may be hurt by the words spoken by the other individual when they were meant to be funny.

- **Find common ground.** Create a list of items that both parties can accept to start the meeting. Then, focus on resolving issues that need to be worked out.

- **Don't be trapped emotionally by the deal.** Even if you are in desperate need of a commission from a given real estate deal, don't react out of fear.

- **Show your high sense of humor, when required.** Humor makes people happy and smile, and hence open-minded and receptive.

- **Focus on your body language.** Look at people in the eye as much as you can to assist them in looking honest and trustworthy.

- **Do close negotiations on a high note**. Before you step out of the room, make sure that everyone feels positive about the results of the real estate negotiation that has just happened. Shake hands, and thank everyone for their contribution, and talk about the next positive steps in the process.

- **Negotiate with data and not opinion.** This does not mean that price negotiation should not happen. Of course, they should—the problem is to find a good price that is reasonable.

- **Incentives can be offered by sellers, too.** There are many types of incentives that a seller can provide, or a buyer can ask in the transaction, and they are all part of the negotiation.

CHAPTER 10:

Secrets to Optimize Your Potential

There are three important factors that, when applied well, will allow you to maximize your potential as it connects to buying and selling houses.

Post Entry Planning

Your post entry approach is the detailed plan of action you will take instantly after the closing of your property. Keep in mind that time is critical, and every day that passes by without being fully used costs you cash. This is the reason why you need to plan well for the closing date for the work needed to prepare the property for its final resale.

Reducing the turnaround time on every deal is important to allow you to optimize your profits.

One of the best methods to start preparing is by scheduling the contractors who will conduct the repairs two to three weeks before the scheduled closing date if possible.

Don't wait until you close to start thinking about scheduling. You will lose important time by doing so, and remember that time is money because you will be paying interest on the borrowed funds.

The right time to start the scheduling process is when the contractors first come out of the property to submit bids for the work performed. This data is used in the inspection of the project viability. Once you consider all the costs related to the project, then and only then can you accurately measure the expected return in profits that a given project will generate.

When you interact with contractors, you can give them a general idea of when you expect to close. Make sure you tell the contractors how relevant it is for them to be present when you need them. Tell them that you prefer not to waste even a single day. Once you have set a closing date with the seller and title company, you can move on to schedule a certain date and time for your contractor to perform the repairs. The goal is to create your post entry plan well in advance and to be ready to implement it as soon after the closing.

DIY vs. Hiring It Out

Do you prefer to do it yourself and save money, or hire someone and save time? This is a question that many investors struggle with, especially those who are just getting started. While there's no specific answer, it is better to understand the pros and cons of both approaches.

For those who would be more mechanically inclined, it is okay to feel and believe that you should do a big percentage of the work yourself in order to save money.

Increasing the Marketability of Your Property

You have worked in the last few weeks or months to improve your investment property. You have increased the value of the house by a great amount, and it is now time to sell it and earn the profit that you have developed. There are several things that you can do to increase the marketability of your property and to raise the exposure it gets. Some of these things include heightened visibility, preplanning, pricing your property competitively, and providing incentives.

Preplanning

Correct planning from the start to the end is important for you to be successful in this business. This involves planning for the sale of your property. After all, you aren't rewarded for your efforts until the sale has been finalized. Only then do you pocket profits from your labors. You could be thinking that you are going to sell a property, but you would be shocked at the number of investors waiting before they reach that stage of selling before they start to think of how they will sell their property.

Equally important is your exit plan. Overall, you need to start thinking about how you are going to sell your property before you buy it. You need to have taken the right steps to create a well-defined sales strategy that you are ready to implement instantly at the right time.

Increasing Visibility Through the MLS

MLS is a great tool that provides your property with the right exposure. How? You list your property for sale with the help of a certified real estate agent unless you are a certified agent yourself. Once your house is listed on the MLS, you earn instant access to hundreds and even thousands of sales agents who have a possible interest in your property. Anyone of them might have a potential buyer with whom they are working who could be interested in exactly what they are selling. You cannot afford to avoid listing any of your property in the MLS. Don't forget that you are running a business of purchasing houses, improving them, and selling them as quickly as possible. Your duty in this business should be that of a manager. You are there to guide the process and make sure that things happen when they are meant to happen.

Trying to sell the house yourself and save money is not different from doing the repairs yourself. While it helps you save money, it can restrict you from achieving your full potential in this business. Thus, if you know that you are not a certified real estate agent, look for an experienced agent who has a proven track record. This means you should find a competent agent who will help you sell your properties quickly.

Selling a Marketable Product

To further increase the marketability of your house, you need to offer a product that people want. As simple as this may appear, this is a vital point that should not be assumed. As an investor, you don't want to stay longer with your inventory. In other words, you need to carefully examine the place in which you want to invest in understanding the vicinities that are highly marketable. The location that is best suitable for selling your houses is probably a neighborhood between 10-30 years old.

These neighborhoods are one where the average middle-class citizen stays. The best location is one in which most properties are well maintained, and that is not suffering from functional obsolescence. The place should be well established, have better schools nearby, and continue to have homes that sell on average in minimum days that those close to communities.

Competitive Pricing

If you study before buying your investment property, you need to be familiar with pricing in your market. It is advised to make your house available for sale at a price slightly lower than the market.

As an investor in the real estate business, you don't have time to sit in your house for an indefinite period trying to hold out for a top dollar. Keep in mind that you have to carry costs, including taxes, insurance, and interest. Therefore, the quicker you sell, the quicker you can get rid of those obligations. Besides, you have an opportunity cost—this means that as long as your investment capital is connected to a single property, you are restricted in your ability to take advantage of other opportunities. Your capital is constrained. Time is money in this business, thus the quicker you are able to sell your house, the more money you can make.

Offering Incentives

If you are like most individuals, chances are you are driven by money. Your potential buyers will become motivated by money too. You can apply various types of incentives that have monetary value to attract potential buyers to buy your house. For example, you can include a credit at closing for landscaping. This will allow buyers to decorate the exterior of their new house shortly after they move in. For most buyers, more specifically first-time buyers, it takes everything they have financially to move in, so they will highly appreciate having something extra during closing. Whether the credit is used for landscaping or another purpose is not important. Your main goal is to offer them a reason to purchase your house now instead of continuing to search for more properties. Other forms of incentives include paying the buyer's closing costs, providing free appliances, or a gift certificate from a local moving company to reduce the moving costs.

This section has looked at the three important factors that when used correctly, will allow you to optimize your potential in the real estate industry. We have looked at different post entry methods, whether to DIY or hire contractors, and various methods to increase your marketability. The three factors explored in this chapter will allow you to grow your potential in the real estate sector. Each of these elements requires time to master. You must be ready to try them, but stay patient as you do so. Life is full of adversities and drawbacks that can test your grit. You must be ready to face these challenges with courage and hope. You must be ready to respond, and not react, to worsen the situation.

When you rise up to conquer whatever challenges that come, then and only then do you win—additionally, then and only then is your personality and moral fiber strengthened.

Building Your Winning Team of Experts

To truly succeed as a real estate investor, you need to gather your team of winning experts. If you are going to buy and sell only one or two properties every year, as it is for most investors, you will do most of the work yourself. However, as you continue to get involved in more and more transactions, you will soon realize that you can no longer do everything on your own. In fact, you will discover that the best use of your time is uniting others' efforts. By delegating some of the tasks to your team, you are able to accomplish more than if you attempt to do everything by yourself.

Scouts/Dealers

Probably the most critical aspect of your winning team of professionals is to have dedicated dealers and scouts working on your behalf. Both dealers and scouts can supply a constant source of property deals. Leads from these sources and other avenues are the powerhouse of your business. Without them, it is going to be very difficult to become successful in the business of flipping properties. You should strive to create relationships with various scouts and dealers. You also need to take time to build an investment criterion that suits your objectives so that the individuals you are working with understand the types of opportunities to present to you. You don't want them to spend countless time on deals that you are not interested in. Besides this, you don't want to waste your time working on deals that don't fulfill your needs.

The relationship between you and scouts is a mutual benefit. The more opportunities they get, the more you will purchase from them or those they suggest, and the more you purchase them, the more money they will generate. It is a win-win kind of relationship. You can also choose to employ a full-time scout of your choice. Besides paying small wages, it is good to establish an incentive system where your scout will be rewarded for every deal he or she brings that you end up purchasing. Your scout will quickly discover the type of opportunities you are highly interested in and bring you only the best.

Office Manager

A great office manager is another important individual on your winning team of experts. Before you get a good office manager, you first need an office. Many people who invest in real estate begin by buying and selling a little at a time. As their capital base increases, so does their potential to increase the volume of transactions. At some point in the process, it will be necessary to end your part-time operation out of your home office and start a full-time operation in your office building.

When you reach this point in your business, it is important that the first people you need to recruit is an office manager. You can delegate many lesser duties to him so that you can save time.

Also, you can train them slowly to handle bigger responsibilities, such as some of the marketing and accounting functions.

A good office manager should also be trained to learn how to perform functions such as coordinating all the relevant parties and scheduling.

Property Rehab Manager

You understand the advantage of a rehab manager. This is the person who will take the rehab out of the rehabbing for you. The main role of the rehab manager is to set up and coordinate subcontractors for all of the required renovations. A handy individual is the most qualified person for this job. You want someone who can manage the crews and understand what needs to be done, and to verify that the repairs have been done perfectly.

A handy person can also save you the costs by doing most of the smaller repairs. However, this depends on the number of properties being worked on at any given time. If you have more than one house being worked one simultaneously, a rehab manager may not have the time to complete any repairs. On the flip side, if you only have two or three in progress at any given time, then your rehab manager will most likely complete some of the repairs while at the same time scheduling other contractors.

Keep in mind that the most effective application of your time is not to repair the houses yourself, but to assess the efforts of those who do. By recruiting a property rehab manager, you are delegating that responsibility to a different person. This provides you time to concentrate on building your business.

Mortgage Broker

Another critical factor of your real estate venture is financing. As such, it is important for you to have one or more mortgage brokers as members of your winning team. You must have access to capital, and preferably to big sources of it. It always becomes important to create relationships with different lenders to fulfill your growing demands.

Real Estate Attorney

Another member of your winning team of professionals that you will want to factor is a real estate attorney.

Yellow Pages have many attorneys who advertise the area of law they specialize in. Get one who is specialized in real estate.

Title Company

A professional title company is another important member of your winning team. Although many title companies provide the same service, they differ highly on the degree to which they can offer those services.

Real Estate Agents

The best real estate agents are key elements of your winning team. You need to plan to have as many as possible on your team. If an agent knows that you are a serious buyer, he or she will try to bring the types of deals you are most interested in.

In summary, each member of your team is critical for your success in real estate. At the start, you may go through a trial and error method where some members of the team have to be replaced for one reason or another. Over time, you will eventually have a team of professionals who work together to help you hit your goals more than you could ever hope to on your own.

Conclusion

We have made to the end of *How to Get Started in Real Estate Investing*.

Buying and selling real estate properties can be one of the most powerful investment methods an individual can take part in. There are many approaches to invest in real estate, as you have seen in this book.

That aside, real estate investing has a lot of benefits. For example, it allows you to own your business, take advantage of appreciation, build positive cash flow, and a lot more.

Apart from the many benefits that real estate provides, there are opportunities for success no matter your financial situation. With real estate, you get the flexibility to set investment choices suitable to your schedule and needs.

As you may know, a lot of information may confuse you, especially if you are a newbie. Hence, I believe the topics covered in this book will give you a strong foundation to get started quickly—and if you get started and keep going, you can overcome those other pesky beginner obstacles.

Since real estate is a broad industry, stay flexible, keep learning, and never be afraid to try new methods that emerge.

www.ingramcontent.com/pod-product-compliance
Lightning Source LLC
Chambersburg PA
CBHW070642220526
45466CB00001B/261